KU-645-039

Contents

Understanding Deception

New Age Teaching in the Church

Roy Livesey

New Wine Press

New Wine Press
P.O. Box 17
Chichester
West Sussex PO20 6YB
England

All quotations are from the Authorised Version Bible.

ISBN 0 947852 29 8

Printed in Great Britain by
Courier International, Tiptree, Essex.

To My Christian Partners

who have supported by their faithful prayers and who have supplied me material — usually exactly the right material at exactly the right time — which has greatly helped my understanding and my labour of writing.

PART THREE : VEHICLES FOR THE NEW AGE IN THE CHURCH; THEIR DESTINATIONS

Introduction

By the Rev. David E. Gardner
(Author of ''The Trumpet Sounds for Britain'')

This book could not be more timely. It has been written to raise the *Alarm!*

It has been written to highlight the *Deception* which abounds in so many sections of the Body of Christ in this Country today. It has been written to show how utterly vital is the need for *Discernment* between the truth and error, between what is a genuine work of God and what is counterfeit. It has been written also to expose what is being infiltrated into the Church and into the churches of our land. Powerful spirits are at work. And we need to be warned about them.

The Alarm Bells, therefore, have been truly set-a-ringing in the pages of this book. And it is not before time.

In my own itinerant ministry all over the Country, and in my own observations of what is going on, I have been made all too aware for some time now that all is not well within many of the sections of the Body of Christ which now exist throughout the land. We have heard it said that the Spirit of God is mightily at work. But I have also been getting the sense that there is something wrong somewhere — that there is also a lot that is phoney going on. One gets the impression that a colossal *mixture* of what is good and what is questionable is being produced. It is something which it is not always easy to put a finger on. But throughout the pages of this book Roy Livesey identifies what it is and brings it right out into the open. Every true believer throughout the land should read, mark, learn, and inwardly digest what he has written in these pages, and then act accordingly.

Questions have often been raised in my own mind, for

instance, about certain things that are going on in the Charismatic Movement which are not necessarily being brought about by the Spirit of Jesus. The Baptism of The Holy Spirit, as spoken of in *Acts Chapter 2* and in other parts of the New Testament, was a very awe-inspiring experience. That spoken of in *Acts Chapter 2* was *spontaneous*. It was God coming down in Holy Ghost Power — very suddenly — on the one hundred and twenty disciples in the Upper Room. For those disciples it was *an enduement with Power from On High*. So much so, that within hours it had had a mighty effect on Jerusalem itself. For immediately Peter and others began to preach amongst the multitude who had come together in the streets to ask what it was that had happened, real conviction of sin resulted, and first three thousand were convicted to Christ, then five thousand, and then a great multitude were convicted, repented and were saved and added to the Church. Nothing even approaching that kind of mighty impact has happened in the Country as a whole, certainly not in its Capital!

Moreover there seems to be a mixture of the real with the counterfeit among those in the Charismatic Movement, which certainly didn't occur on the original Day of Pentecost. So one is obliged to ask, "What really *is* this?" We now have Roman Catholics claiming that the "Baptism in The Spirit" has made "the worship of Mary" more meaningful to them; and that it has made "The Mass" more meaningful to them, and that it leads to a greater veneration of the Pope etc!

The question arises "How can this be?" since the Holy Ghost, being the Spirit of *Truth,* and being *HOLY,* cannot possibly condone error. "How can this be?" when the Scripture says *"Be ye not unequally yoked together with unbelievers: for what fellowship hath righteousness with unrighteousness? and what communion hath light with darkness? 2 Corinthians 6:14.* Rather the call is to come out (Revelation 18:4).

I have come to the conclusion that there must also be *another* spirit at work in the Charismatic Movement which is definitely *not* the Spirit of Jesus, even if the Holy Spirit

2

is *also* at work. And if this is so, that *other* spirit must be a *deceiving* spirit which is at work, a spirit of antichrist. This is where Roy Livesey points out there is real need for *discernment*.

This serves to remind us that the Bible quite plainly shows that Satan desires to produce his counterfeit. Roy Livesey gives illustration after illustration throughout these pages of how this is true, and that *this* is, in fact, what is happening in our churches today. There are *powerful spirits* at work introducing all kinds of *deception,* sometimes of the most subtle kind. The greatest need amongst Christians and Christian leaders, therefore, is for *discernment* which is so sadly lacking in the Church today.

It is not only in the "Charismatic Realm" that this kind of thing is happening. The Body of Christ all over the Country is being infiltrated by false spirits who are bringing in false teaching. Roy Livesey points out that tragically there is much that is not right in the Church and in the churches. Not all in the Body of Christ is of God. The Lord is at work, yes. Souls are being saved, yes. But there is *another* spirit also at work which is not the Spirit of Jesus. Almost unbelievable deception is taking place. Most subtle teaching is being introduced which is either a distortion of what the Word of God says, or a subtle departure from it. We are dealing with a wave of deception of the worst degree. Roy Livesey asks if this is *"the strong delusion"* which the Apostle Paul speaks about in 2 Thessalonians 2:11.

Ministers, Pastors, Christian Leaders, Churches, and individual Christians are seen to be going "off course" as a result of the false and unbiblical teaching which is infiltrating the churches in the United Kingdom, and through sheer lack of knowledge of what the Bible as a whole teaches, particularly about the things related to "The Coming Age". And much of this false and distorted teaching is coming from America! So every Christian in the Country needs to be well and truly alerted and put on their guard. The Body of Christ throughout the Country is being well and truly infiltrated by false, distorted, and erroneous doctrines which are coming

3

from across the Atlantic.

Roy Livesey lists a number of these strange and sometimes alluring doctrines. He evaluates the distortions in: "Prosperity Teaching;" "Positive Thinking;" "The Positive Mental Attitude" Movement: "The Positive Confession" Movement: "Inner Healing" which has occult involvement within it, and in its origins; those "Signs and Wonders" which also have the element of the occult within them and in some of their methods, techniques, and practices; The Doctrine of Self-Esteem; Shepherding/Discipleship and "Establishing The Kingdom" Teaching.

He points out that there is a measure of truth in all of these, but also shows what the measure of error is, from where it stems, and how it deviates from the Bible.

There is an urgent need of a Watchman, first to see what is going on, and then to *warn*.

It is not false doctrines and false teachings alone which are infiltrating the churches. It is also very questionable use of "methods," "systems" and "teachings" in order to bring about "results" which is causing so much confusion. "Word-power", psychology, psychiatry, "mind-control", "mind-power", and mind-manipulating techniques, hypnosis and the like are considered acceptable. "Mind-power" can be used at mass meetings and in the churches, and especially in the "healing" ministries, where the introduction of "mind-centred" ideas are given Christian labels under the disguise of the "inner healing". Hinduism, and "methods", "systems" and "techniques" connected with Eastern Religions are even being used, maybe unknowingly at times. In fact, what is being looked at in this book is *Man's* attempts to build a system of techniques and methods that have been known to occultists for thousands of years.

"Mind over matter" doctrines are also being introduced and used. Roy Livesey points out from his own experience that "mind-power" is very much at work in many healing techniques which are being used in many churches and ministries today. And he points out that such healing power is often a demon power at work. "The question that needs to be asked is *not, "Does it work?" but "By what Power are the 'results' being brought about?"* Or *"Which Power is at work?"* When facing up to all this, the question we need to ask is:— How does all this compare with what we see happening in the New Testament?

We read in Matthew 9:25 that Jesus went about .... *"healing every sickness and every disease"*. But *how* did He do it? Not by "methods", not by "techniques", not by "systems", not by the use of hypnosis or mind-controlling ideas, and certainly not by "visualisation" and "getting pictures", or by "the healing of memories". The New Testament tells us precisely *how* it was that He did it. It specifically states, how *"God anointed Jesus of Nazareth with* **the Holy Ghost** *and with power: who went about doing good, and healing all that were oppressed with the devil; for God was with Him."* Acts 10:38. He didn't resort to techniques and methods in order to bring about results. He said, *"If I by* **The Spirit of God** *cast out devils, then know that the kingdom of God has come upon you."*

It was *by The Holy Spirit* that He did it. He did it by the Power of The Holy Ghost, not by using techniques. We don't find the Apostles in the New Testament resorting to any of these "methods" or techniques when they wrought miracles of healing. What happened in the Lord Jesus Christ's case and in the Apostle's case, is what should be applying today if we want to see a real work of God being done in our churches.

Yet who is it who has taken on board all this false teaching, distorted doctrines, and wrong emphasis? It is not the Established Church. The Established Church is guilty of a different form of apostasy. The apostasy of the Established Church has taken the form of reversing all that God brought about in the Reformation and then going all out for union with the Roman Catholic Church at the expense of basic New Testament doctrines and teachings. Some of its Bishops and Archbishops have been denying the Virgin Birth, the physical and actual Resurrection of Our Lord Jesus Christ, His actual, visible, personal return and talking about God

5

being a God *other* than the God of the Bible.

Roy Livesey makes it plain that it is not the apostasy of the Established Church that this book sets out to expose. It is written for those who have fallen for all the false teaching and emphasis which he highlights in this book.

It is due to their accepting either a direct departure from Scripture, a subtle turning away from Scripture, a complete distortion of what the Scripture actually says, or the introduction of some "new revelation" said to be coming from God, some "extra-Biblical revelation" or some going *beyond* Scripture and beyond what Scripture says.

Roy Livesey quite rightly points out, "There are movements afoot today which, while continuing to identify themselves with fundamental Christianity, in fact teach contrary to it". He does valuable work in tracing this kind of teaching right back to its origins. He is anxious to get right at its roots, as he does in the case of so many *other* aspects of false teaching which has infiltrated the Church of God today. And once again much seems to come from America.

Just as it is true that the *Holy* Spirit of God is at work preparing The Bride of Christ for the personal return of The Lord Jesus Christ — so it is true that there is a powerful and deceiving spirit at work preparing the world for the emergence of the Anti-Christ — and preparing the Anti-Christ's Counterfeit Kingdom of Satan.

And the strategy of *that* powerful and deceiving spirit is to bring about a so-called "unity" to the world. It is to unite the world in One. And so we are seeing that spirit today working to bring about unity between capitalism and communisim — unity between East and West, unity between governments, unity between all the world's monetary systems, unity in world trade, unity and so-called "reconciliation" between nations, unity between the Church of England, the Free Churches and the Church of Rome, and unity between all the other faiths and religions of the world and the re-constituted One-World Church with the Pope as its Head. It is a strategy of *One Colossal Merger*.

Hence there are forces at work today to bring about through

the means of creating this so-called ''unity'', and motivated
by that spirit of Anti-christ to bring into being a One-World
Church comprising all the faiths and religions of the world,
a One-World Religion, a One-World Economic System and
a One-World Government. And when that One-World
Government has been established it must ultimately and
inevitably result in a One-World Ruler emerging to head up
that One-World Government. And the Bible makes it crystal-
clear that *that* One-World Ruler will be the Beast of the Book
of The Revelation, namely the Anti-Christ who is to rule over
all the kingdoms of this world in this counterfeit Kingdom
of Satan.

In this process which is already very much in being,
''unity'' is the ''in'' word and ''Merger'' is another key
word. We see all kinds of mergers taking place today. The
idea is that everything must be merged into One. And all
obstacles standing in the way of that ''unity'' taking place,
and of that ''merging into One'' being achieved must be
totally removed and be done away with.

We can see, for instance, the Ecumenical Movement hard
at work bringing about the merger into a One-World Church
of The Church of England and the other church denominations under the leadership of the Pope of Rome, and of the
Church of Rome. But how many have seen that the two recent
Popes and the non-charismatic hierarchy and authority in the
Church of Rome have been actively encouraging the Charismatic Movement and those members of the Roman Catholic
Church who have participated in that Movement and who
have themselves become charismatics in order to launch a
new Roman Catholic strategy aimed at uniting what was lost
in the Reformation and at bringing the Protestants to Rome,
as a major part of an ecumenical movement towards one-
world religion with the Pope at its head? We can also see
the Movement aimed at the syncretisation of all the other
faiths and religions of the world hard at work, and being
manifest in this Country by such functions as Commonwealth
Services in Westminster Abbey in the presence of The
Queen, who is the temporal Head of The Church of England,

when Hindus, Sikhs, Buddhists and Muslims actually take part in the 'Services'. These are all mergers which are taking place right now.

The idea is abroad, and certainly prevails among charismatics that we must never divide over doctrinal issues for the sake of ''unity''. It must be unity at all costs — even at the expense of basic doctrine. The issues of basic Christian doctrine stand in the way of unity. They are barriers to a merger taking place. Therefore such barriers must be removed and must be done away with. Similarly, the idea is abroad and is prevailing in charismatic and in these other realms that we should never judge other believers, even though they may be seen to hold views that are blatantly contrary to Scripture. A liberal ''tolerance policy'' has been developed as a means of ''bridging'' the traditional, doctrinal gap which exists between the various denominations which individual charismatics continue to represent. ''Suppress doctrinal differences'' is the cry in order to establish our Oneness. But it is a false Oneness, a false merger.

But this is also the policy which is being adopted and developed so as to ''bridge the gap'' between the Church of England and the Church of Rome. *That* is what is going on in the ARCIC Conferences and Debates. The essential truth of the Gospel is being suppressed in order to bring about the MERGER of the two Churches. It is also the policy which has been developed in order to ''bridge the gap'' between Christianity and the other faiths and religions of the world. It is called in all these cases ''the policy of tolerance'' in order to bring about a Oneness between all.

But it is a *false* spirit which is at work. This can most clearly be seen by what happened at the 1975 Congress of Charismatic Renewal at the Vatican. It happened during the Celebration of the Eucharist in St. Peter's Basilica with Pope Paul stepping to his throne. It was stated that it was a new Pentecost which took place. But the question needs to be asked, ''Does The Holy Spirit condone and authenticate the Pope's claim to be The Vicar of Christ on Earth when it is

The Holy Spirit Himself who occupies that position? Does The Holy Spirit condone and authenticate the Pope's title as "The Holy Father", when God Almighty is the *only* Holy Father that there is? Does the Holy Spirit condone and authenticate the worship of Mary, and the practice of praying to Mary when the Scriptures specifically declare that Jesus is the One and Only Mediator between God and man? Does the Holy Spirit condone and authenticate the Roman Catholic sacrifice of the Mass when Jesus Himself has already made the one, all-sufficient sacrifice to atone for the sins of the whole world?''

This could never have been the descent of the *Holy* Spirit in terms of a New Pentecost, otherwise the *Holy* Spirit would be condoning and authenticating what the teaching of Scripture, which He Himself brought into being, is totally and absolutely against. It must have been some *other* spirit which descended — a totally deceiving spirit. Those who move in Charismatic Circles and seek to go into Renewal need discernment enough to recognise and realise this, when you have an unregenerate Church.

So there are these powerful forces at work in the world today, led by a spirit of antichrist, bringing about a One-World Church, a One-World religion and a One-World Government in order to pave the way for a One-World Ruler — the Anti-Christ — and to pave the way for Satan's Counterfeit Kingdom under the rulership of the Anti-Christ.

Roy Livesey sees the process of merging and uniting everything into One to be taking place in two Camps:

One Camp embraces all those *other* New Age groups, focusing on the creation not the Creator, and which are at work in the world to bring about such things as a One-World Monetary System, a One-World Trading System, a One-World Government and such like.

The *other* Camp comprises Christians who are wrongly and unscripturally set on "building the Kingdom" on Earth under the illusion that they themselves have got to do it before the Lord Jesus Christ can return physically and in person.

The Christian believers in this *second* Camp also see a New

Age Dawning. But it is not the New Age which The Bible talks about — the Messianic Age — which The Bible describes as *"The Times of The Restitution of All Things"* — Acts 3:21 and which the Lord Jesus *Himself* will usher in when He returns. *Their* New Day which they see dawning is a day of earthly peace and prosperity. So they prophesy great and prosperous times ahead. *Their* concern, therefore, is to bring in a bright New Day of endless prosperity and bliss, and boast that God is going to give us the wealth of the world; we will become kings — take dominion over all government, all science, all law and legislation, all nature. So their leaders, with great zeal, are encouraging and urging their supporters to get involved in governments, into local councils, into school management, and into positions of authority *now,* not with the Scriptural idea of being "the salt of the earth" and the "light of the world" but with the motive of doing this in order that they themselves might bring in the kingdom and "take the world for Jesus" *before* He can return.

But it is a *false* Gospel, and a complete distortion of the true Gospel and of all the End-Day Prophecies of The Bible.

The serious danger which Roy Livesey sees likely to take place is that those forces which are at work to bring in the Kingdom of the Anti-Christ will be joining up with the believing "Kingdom-Builders" as they work to bring in a Utopia here on earth — and that the believing "Kingdom-Builders" will be sucked in to the other group. And because they are looking forward to the wrong kind of "New Age", such Christian believers will suddenly wake up to the fact that they have been drawn into the wrong camp and the wrong Kingdom by a colossal deception and by the subtle infiltration of false and unbiblical teaching. He gives out a strong warning about this and sees the very real possibility of this happening.

Roy Livesey writes "The Kingdom people therefore are not far from these counter-parts in the other Camp" — the one comprising those who are building what will eventually be the Kingdom of the Anti-Christ. It could easily lead to a *merger*.

The *warning* needs to be sounded, and Roy Livesey is sounding that warning loud and clear. There is much that needs to be exposed, and Roy is bringing it right out into the open. Believers certainly need to keep an eye on what is coming from America. They need to be extremely wary lest they be taken in by it all. And Roy is certainly alerting all Believers about that.

He writes, "This book is to encourage the reader in his own discernment, and discernment is desperately needed in the Body of Christ today." Furthermore, all that he exposes and brings to light reveals how vitally important it is to know the Bible, the *whole* of the Bible.

Never was there a time either, when it was so vitally important to stress that it is The Bible which is our authority — our *only* authority, and that it is The Bible plus *nothing*. Not the Bible plus tradition, or the Bible as interpreted by some church's "Magistarium" or "Shepherd". It is the Bible itself and the Bible *alone* which is our Court of Appeal — our *sole* Court of Appeal. Never was it so important to stress either, that we must never go beyond what the Bible says or teaches, and never be led astray by so-called "extra-Biblical Revelation", "New" Revelation or "Progressive Revelation". We must not be taken in, either, by such things as, hearing "a voice", "feeling a presence", seeing "auras", "seeing pictures", or the type of language and phraseology which talks about diagnosing diseases by "vibrations in the hand" or that has anything to do with "visualisation" — all of which things can, and do often have, occult and demonic connections and are due to *another* spirit which is not the Spirit of Jesus. These things have infiltrated the Body of Christ in strength today. Even the practice of "hearing God" should be checked biblically — because it is terribly possible to hear somebody who is *other* than God, whilst seeking to hear God.

The alarm bells need to be rung, and Roy Livesey is ringing them loud and clear throughout this book.

The Church today needs to be well and truly *alerted* and

11

Roy Livesey is doing the *alerting*.

All true believers need to have their eyes opened to what is happening, and Roy Livesey is well and truly *opening their eyes*.

A stern warning needs to be issued about so much that is coming from America, and Roy Livesey is issuing that warning.

This book is a veritable Handbook. He has faithfully checked all his facts. He has diligently traced false and unbiblical teachings to their original source, and has sought to get at their very roots. He has totally exposed and brought right out into the open so much that urgently needs to be exposed.

All Ministers, Pastors, Christian Leaders and all true Believers urgently need to set themselves the task of reading this book at least three or four times over, in order to get a firm grasp of what Roy is saying. They need to read, mark, learn, and inwardly digest the book's contents and then act drastically on what they discover from it.

Powerful spirits are indeed at work in our churches and in the world itself intent on deceiving many, and, if it were possible, even the very elect. *Discernment* is therefore urgently needed.

This book will help give all who read and study it that necessary *discernment*.

Preface

Jesus gave a WARNING. To some who worked *in His name* He will say "I never knew you." It is a warning that should encourage our discernment so that we may know the difference between truth and error spoken in His name. Encouraged and not dismayed by that warning, I have written this book to highlight the deception that abounds in the body of believers, to help towards the discernment necessary and to invite readers to be *lovers* of the truth. In 2 Thessalonians 2:10 Paul writes of attitudes. We need to *love* the truth. We may not know all the truth, but if we *love* the truth the Holy Spirit can take us on into more turth. I believe this *love* of the truth is something that many believers do not have. Let them heed Jesus's *warning* and know that Jesus Himself, the Word, the truth, is our safeguard. Jesus *warned:*

> *Not everyone that saith unto me, Lord, Lord, shall enter into the kingdom of heaven; but he that doeth the will of my Father which is in heaven.*
>
> *Many will say to me in that day, Lord, Lord, have we not prophesied in thy name? and in thy name have cast out devils? and in thy name done many wonderful works?*
>
> *And then will I profess unto them, I never knew you; depart from me, ye that work iniquity.*
>
> (Matthew 7:21—23)

Many will say that this scripture doesn't apply to them. They will point to spiritualists, the miracle workers in the cults and all the rest. It is the urgent suggestion of this book that the above scripture presents a timely warning to all who are indeed blinded by Satan through their involvement with practices which belong to the New Age, the idea that Man is a god, and mind power.

Jesus is preparing His bride. At this same time the bride

13

for the Antichrist is being prepared, the New Age Movement. This book deals with its infiltration into the Church.

Previous books, "Understanding Alternative Medicine", "Understanding the New Age", and "New Age to New Birth", deal fairly adequately with the impact of the New Age on secular society. However, much in the areas covered has overspilled into the body of Christ. The popular therapy homoeopathy, so-called "Christian" Rock music and C.S. Lewis's "Chronicles of Narnia" books are good examples. However what we are concerned with in this book is to contend for the faith (Jude 3) and discern *some* false doctrines that have become the focus of *some* Christian ministries.

It could be unhelpful to the reader in many cases if I do not mention the name of the ministry referred to. By my own choice I have limited the use of names where possible, but contend that the Apostles spoke specifically of men who were not teaching the word of God correctly. In no case of course is there any sense of judging individuals. It will be pointed out that many in the ministries in each group I have referred to see many souls led to Christ. However it is by their fruits we shall know them. Satan is given entrance through the serious doctrinal errors on which I shall be focusing. He will have his fruits too, and those not discerning the error may not discern the bad fruit. The Bible speaks of Satan's wiles; he has a plan and has been around a long time! How many are blinded to Rome by "teaching"? How many are blinded to the true role of the Jews and Israel? How many are blinded to the occult and the rest of the New Age as the result of "teaching" or of the soul-winning "Rock and Pop" altar calls? Many of today's preachers are blinded by the enemy; did they fall into compromise and error and cease to love the truth at some stage in their Christian battle? Mostly they are very sincere men, often totally committed to the Lord.

For we wrestle not against flesh and blood, but against principalities, against powers, against the rulers of the darkness of this world, against spiritual wickedness in high places. (Ephesians 6:12)

The battle against error and heresy is an enormous subject.

I deal only with those areas I believe the Lord has shown *me*. They are errors that struck *me* one at a time after leaving behind my old life as a New Ager and ending my time as a "searcher" in the occult realm. First I had to receive Jesus into my life and realise that I had been following a New Age path. That was five years ago.

What I write about I have mostly met and not just read about. They are errors which find common ground with the New Age and the occult. They are errors shared, not with the atheist unbelievers, the products of the materialist society; that common ground is taken by the professing-but-dead Church. The Church we look at is one that is very far from dead; the errors we look at are those of our time, perhaps potentially more dangerous. They are errors which find common ground with the spiritually minded in other religions and who have experience of the supernatural. They are errors which find focus in the lie that is as old as the Garden of Eden — the serpent's lie that we can be as gods (Genesis 3:5). They are errors that are increasingly taken on board and promoted by Christian men with renewed spirits, but with passive rather than renewed minds (Romans 12:2). They are errors that the spirit of Antichrist is using to build his kingdom. They are errors which serve to narrow the gap which separates the false message of the "kingdom" (the kingdom on earth here and now established by men) and the message of the New Age movement.

It is absolutely necessary in these end times that we should be alerted to the false; it starts off so like the true. I trust this book may encourage us to examine our beliefs and to understand that we *can* — new Christians and great men of God alike — be deceived. It is an encouragement to examine our beliefs and to expose anything which is false when measured against the authority of Scripture.

Many may properly ask what are the *ways of the Lord* as they identify themselves with deceptions mentioned throughout the book. I endeavour to set the positive alongside the negative. However the effective answers, the alternatives, are to be found only as we anchor in Jesus. Indeed we can throw out Satan's deceptions as we discern them, and we may trust in the Lord to lead us. All of the answers are in His Word.

Nevertheless effective answers are called for and it is in the particular nature of the deceptions dealt with in the following pages that it is right to emphasise *two* areas.

First, there needs to be a death to the self-life. In chapter two we shall see how the notion that "ye are as gods" has a grip in so much of the error. We need to get the victory over sin and to crucify the flesh. Jesse Penn-Lewis tells us how we can move in Spirit with the Lord: "Just as the Lord was put to death on Calvary, and quickened in the Spirit, so you must go to Calvary and in spiritual meaning 'be put to death in the flesh'. The flesh must be accounted crucified (Galatians 5:24) so that the believer may 'walk by the spirit' day by day, and not fulfil the desires of the flesh (Galatians 5:16,25)."* That's going back to basics but for many of us it's the place where we have to look.

Speaking at a leaders' Convention in 1910 Jesse Penn-Lewis referred to the warfare that most of us have known, personal temptation and how to get victory over sin. She ventured that this ought to be a matter already settled by those who are in God's service.

The *second* area that needs to be emphasised here is that of the spiritual warfare. In chapter three we consider the passivity which paves the way to so much deception. Having conquered the flesh and risen off the earthly ground, there are many souls with their hearts sold out to God who fail to recognise the principalities and powers of the enemy arrayed against them (Ephesians 6:12). They do not know from scripture that a life victorious over self and sin needs to engage the enemy and be victorious in warfare. If we don't engage the enemy, he will engage us. We have to put on all the armour of God for the battle. Deceptions — subtle deceptions — will be Satan's way with Christians.

Let us ask the Lord to give us discernment and to quicken

* "Life in the Spirit" by Jesse Penn-Lewis (1910) (The Overcomer Literature Trust, 10, Marlborough Road, Parkstone, Poole, Dorset BH14 0HJ)

the truth of His Word to us. Let us pray that we may recognise every deception that the enemy sends our way. Let us be on our guard against those teachings that lead us to experiences but not to repentance.

What follows in the pages of this book is one man's attempt to encourage that discernment. I have sought to check out what I have written both against the Word and with the understanding of men of God far more capable than I. In Proverbs 15:22 we read:

Without counsel purposes are disappointed: but in the multitude of counsellors they are established.

The book is not intended to be controversial. In Romans 14 Paul acknowledges there will be differences. These will not be harmful if we accept one another, love one another and continue to dig into the only book — the Bible — in order that we can at least become convinced in our own minds on that basis. My own books don't have such authority! Aside from controversy, I prefer to say I could be wrong. Rather my prayer is that by airing the deceptions I believe God has shown me, I shall bring no confusion. I encourage others to hear the Lord for themselves as we all must do.

If this were a book about worldly deception rather than deception having its special origin in the heavenly realm, it is interesting to compare the position from which I would be writing. I would be writing from the perspective of the crime reporter; also of one who has been himself involved in misdemeanours. The Police, and the public called to support them, have a different perspective; the lawyers have another. Finally the Judge, well informed as to the law, and with all the authority, has the best view of all.

Thus it is that I write as one who has been involved, both in the New Age and the New Age deceptions in the Church. Involvement in crime, even in crime reporting, is not recommended, and the parallel is drawn with my involvement with the deceptions I describe. I do this as faithfully as I can, yet what I bring to the readers' notice is clearly within the limits of my own understanding. Continuing the analogy, among my readers will be those like policemen and public,

Christian leaders well experienced in some of the areas I bring to notice and ordinary believers, all clear in their knowledge of the Word. I do not offer myself as the policeman, nor as the lawyer or judge. I am neither trained in the way of the theologian, nor do I come as one judging others. I write like the reporter, a reporter who has faithfully checked his stories as well as need be, a reporter who has not ignored the advice of Christians around him, a reporter with the Bible in his hand.

Part One

The Deception and the Cause

1

Keeping an Eye on the Church in the United States

I hardly read the newspapers any more, yet writing about the end-times I needed to keep well informed. We had no TV yet somehow I was better informed than I had ever been before. Then one morning, after I had been a Christian for three years, a quick glance at a morning paper was to have a special result.

As a New Ager more than twenty years earlier I had been involved with the United Nations Association and visited the UN building in New York. Now I was writing about the New Age and I had a chapter about the United Nations in my book "Understanding the New Age" which was pretty well complete. That morning a half-page newspaper advertisement caught my attention. It read "London-Detroit £55 : London-Glasgow £65". It was a "Special Offer" to launch a new London-Detroit non-stop service. Perhaps the first thing that came to my mind was to travel on to New York. I would check out a few things at the United Nations. Much I had discovered, looking at the UN in the light provided by the Holy Spirit, was quite extraordinary. I was soon wading through my correspondence file to see who I knew in New York. I had mountains of correspondence with Christians, including Americans, but no-one in New York!

Then in a new light I remembered a letter I had received from Constance Cumbey, the author of "The Hidden Dangers of the Rainbow". Hers was an eye-opening book on the New Age. I had never heard of the New Age by that name until I visited America the previous year. There I had noticed rainbows everywhere! And it was there that I was recommended to get "The Hidden Dangers of the Rainbow".* I remembered that the book's author lived in Detroit.

I made contact with Constance very easily by telephone. I was invited to stay in her home in Detroit and to check out a few things on the New Age with her. I planned to stay in America for *seven* days and I arrived in Detroit with a Greyhound Return ticket, Detroit-New York. I never did go to New York! I never did set foot in the United Nations there. The Lord had quite a different plan.

"You don't have a god in you; you are one"

Certainly I learned a great deal about the New Age as I listened to Constance, as I dipped into some of the thousands of books on the subject in her library, and as I watched some quite extraordinary films and listened to what seemed unbelievable tapes. On one of these tapes I heard the words: "You don't have a god in you; you are one". It soon became clear that the Lord had got me there to show me just how deeply the New Age had infiltrated the Church. The words "You don't have a god in you; you are one" were not spoken by one of the cult leaders nor by one normally associated with the occult or the mind sciences. It was spoken by one who I considered my favourite "faith" teacher.

The confirmation for my visit to America came about in an interesting way. My finances were very depressed and for the past three months, encouraged by issues of this "Faith" ministry's monthly magazine that majored on the prosperity teaching, I had been taking a more careful look at the "Prosperity Scriptures". Then I received a telephone call from a friend. It was quite out of the blue and he told

* "The Hidden Dangers of the Rainbow" by Constance E. Cumbey (Huntington House, Shreveport, Louisana — 1983)

22

me: "I thought I should tell you, the Lord has shown me that the teaching is from the spirit of Antichrist." When I rang him back a few days later we prayed and he said the Lord gave him a scripture. It was Ezekiel 3:6. It meant nothing to me as I read: *"Not to many people of a strange speech and of a hard language, whose words thou canst not understand"*. Some days later we met and he asked me: 'Did you read on to verse fifteen; you're going to America for *seven* days aren't you?' The enormous significance of Ezekiel 3:6 as the central verse of the whole chapter was still to become clear, but it was true, I was going to America for *seven* days. I welcomed the scripture reference to 'seven' days. I was starting to look at Ezekiel 3. I wasn't familiar with the correct exegesis but I believe the Lord had got my attention!*

It was not surprising that I left for America with my favourite "Faith" teacher very much on my heart. Two more American teachers were on my heart but in a different way because I could see clearly that *they* were in serious error. As for my "Faith" teacher, apart from what my friend had said, I had no bad witness at all and I hadn't yet seen or heard of the tape that was to tell me I was a god. I assess the prosperity teaching in the new light that began to dawn in America in chapter five. The second ministry for my concern was an Inner Healing ministry which focused in a book that was being used by some in our own fellowship. We look at Inner Healing in chapter seven.

The third American teacher for whom I had been burdened was one who had been well received in Britain on recent tours. I had spotted the name of a known occult healer profiled in his teaching materials as an example of those working "Signs and Wonders". My burden was quite simply to reach this teacher with some encouragement to seek the Lord for some real discernment. As with many teachers this was plainly lacking but it seemed especially serious when evidenced in an international ministry that, in Britain at any rate, was getting the attention of such large numbers of

* "New Age to New Birth — A Personal Testimony of Two Kingdoms" by Roy and Rae Livesey (New Wine Press — 1986) — chapter nineteen

Christians.

"Son of Man, I have made Thee a Watchman" (Ezekiel 3:17)

As I left for America it seemed these might be things I would share but I never dreamed that the main concern of seven days in Detroit would be on the New Age infiltration of the Body of Christ. On my arrival Ezekiel chapter three came alive. I had not been sent *"to many people of a strange speech and of a hard language"* (Ezekiel 3:6) but to the house of Israel, not to the New Agers whose esoteric language could be difficult indeed, nor to the church-going unbelievers whose traditions and rituals could be similarly difficult, but it seemed I was also needing to confront on important foundational and fundamental questions some of those whose teaching I had heard and for whom I still had a high personal regard. The three well known names from America were clear examples; there were many others who were little known, some who were near-to-home and some whom I even knew very well. Certainly I wasn't being sent to peoples whose words *"thou canst not understand"* (Ezekiel 3:6).

My countrymen in exile seemed to be these teachers from America (verse 11) *"and I sat where they sat, and remained there astonished among them for seven days"* (verse 15) *"And it came to pass at the end of seven days, that the word of the Lord came unto me saying, Son of Man, I have made thee a watchman unto the house of Israel therefore hear the word at my mouth, and give them warning from me"* (Ezekiel 3:16—17). God called Ezekiel to be a watchman to the house of Israel in order to warn them of the coming judgment on the nation. (Ezekiel 3:15—21). In Old Testament times a watchman's job was to keep a keen eye open for attacks coming up on the horizon outside, and to watch out for fires, riots and disturbances from within. Ezekiel's main task seems to have been as a watchman to warn of the imminent judgment of God upon Israel. He could see it on the horizon.

24

In this regard Ezekiel must have appeared more gloomy and critical than those false prophets who failed in their responsibility to warn Israel. Are these not to be found among Christians today just as they existed among the Jews who Ezekiel wrote about?*

At the end of my stay in America God was saying very clearly they *are* to be found amongst us.

The Lord has impressed upon me the relevance of the second and third chapters of Ezekiel for today when so many Christians are preoccupied with signs and wonders. I waited in the airport hotel for my plane to London. I prayed: "Lord as I get up and go out to the plane, please speak to me." It was a normal prayer of mine for the Lord to have His way and His choice of the person in the next seat beside me. This time Ezekiel 3:22 raised my expectancy. There sitting next to me on the aeroplane was a man travelling from the church of the "Signs and Wonders" ministry for which I was burdened. The Boeing 747 is a very big aeroplane and it was full. This man was travelling from California via Detroit. The Lord *did* speak to me on the plane. His message was extraordinarily clear. Already He had shown me very clearly that there was widespread and deep New Age infiltration of the Church. Yet He was interested in individuals too, and there flowed from that meeting in the air a personal exchange of correspondence with the signs and wonders teacher for whom my travelling companion was working, leading to him changing his teaching material.

I see now how as an enthusiastic and relatively new Christian I was excessively zealous as I slotted many of my experiences in America into chapter three of Ezekiel. It is true that I saw God appointed a watchman in the days when Israel needed warning, and I felt God was leading me similarly in view of what I had found infiltrating the Church.

It is a theme running through this book that Man seeks to be as God. It was this which brought Eve's downfall and the world with her. It is this that tempts Man to add to God's

* "New Age to New Birth"

word. Let us not confuse negative and positive! Many today are applying the word "negative" to those who seek to correct error and bring people back to the Bible whereas "positive" should apply. The same people, usually those who will not hear, *seek* to be "positive" and usually carry the flag for extra-biblical revelation. Many have not actually heard the words of the "Faith" teacher, "You don't have a god in you; you are one." However our battle is in the spiritual realm, not against flesh and blood (Ephesians 6:10) and however hidden, *that* is the message of the powerful spirit at work to bring the New Age into the Church. We find that spirit and that message at work in many of the ministries identified with the false teaching we look at in this book.

I returned from America with the idea of writing this book and with more material than I could use. Some months later the book "The Seduction of Christianity"* provided a much appreciated detailed confirmation of my conclusions. Man aspired to godhood in the New Age and that lie was fast taking hold in the Church.

We are, as Matthew Henry says, "viceroys" with the job of doing *only* what the King says we are to do. As redeemed people we are the clearest looking glass to be found in nature. Jesus was perfect and we are to seek to be like Him; if we don't follow Him and look after ourselves on that basis, then as in a defective looking glass the image will be less clearly seen. The more we allow ourselves to be changed from what is God's design by conforming to the world, and the less we look to Jesus, the more inadequate will we become in reflecting Him. Yet as Christians with God's grace and God's word we are equipped to keep ourselves in good shape so that God *can* be seen in us.

We are made in the image of God — Father, Son and Holy Ghost (Genesis 1:26); not to be another God but to reflect God and allow *Him* to be seen through us. It is not we who are to be "as gods"; that is the lie of the serpent.

* "The Seduction of Christianity — Spiritual Discernment in the Last Days" by Dave Hunt and T.A. McMahon (Harvest House 1985)

2

"Ye Are as gods"

I returned from America with the tape of my favourite "Faith" teacher. Back home, the first meeting was at one of our regular House Groups. The attendance was unusually small and it comprised, I thought, exactly the right people with whom I could check out and share the message I had brought back. Also I was able to play the tape which said "You don't have a god in you; you are one."

There was very little comment and reaction. Then after the meeting was over a friend came alongside me and shared her certainty that we *are* gods. "The Bible says so," she told me.

I hadn't looked at any scripture to check whether I was a god or not. It had hardly seemed necessary! I had been at one time a "searcher" in the occult realm and was familiar with cults where the idea of man as a god is quite normal, but until I heard the tape I had never come across any Christian perspective on the idea. Now one of our close Christian friends was telling me that 'I *am* a god!' (Elohim).

"Elohim" — An Opportunity for Confusion

It took quite a lot of study and reading before I sorted out the different interpretations involving ELOHIM that were presented to me. I found ELOHIM did not always mean "god".

Certainly it was necessary to go back to the original

27

Hebrew word and its translations, but as I look back, the main problem was by no means the intellectual one. *"We wrestle not against flesh and blood but against principalities, against powers"* (Ephesians 6:12). I shall return to the battle I personally had for the grasp of this word ELOHIM. It is a battle the serpent continually brings as he tirelessly tempts us to godhood. This temptation to the idea "ye are as gods", and the defeats of so many in the battle, have given rise to the false teachings that make books like this one necessary. However we first need to take a look at the scriptures.

Scriptures about "God" and Different Meanings of "Elohim"

At the outset it is valuable to read some relevant scriptures about "God" and see some different meanings for the word ELOHIM.

In the beginning God (Elohim) *created the heaven and the earth.* (Genesis 1:1)

For God doth know that in the day ye eat thereof, then your eyes shall be opened, and ye shall be as gods (Elohim), *knowing good and evil.* (Genesis 3:5)

Thus saith the Lord the King of Israel, and his redeemer the Lord of hosts; I am the first, and I am the last; and beside me there is no God." (Isaiah 44:6)

I have said, Ye are gods (Elohim); *and all of you are children of the most High.*

But ye shall die like men, and fall like one of the princes.

Arise, O God, judge the earth: for thou shalt inherit all nations. (Psalm 82:6—8)

What is man, that thou art mindful of him? and the son of man, that thou visitest him?

For thou hast made him a little lower than the angels (Elohim), *and hast crowned him with glory and honour.*

Thou madest him to have dominion over the works of thine hands; thou hast put all things under his feet: (Psalm 8:4—6)

But the Lord is the true God, he is the living God, and an everlasting king: at his wrath the earth shall tremble, and the nations shall not be able to abide his indignation

Thus shall ye say unto them, The gods that have not made the heavens and the earth, even they shall perish from the earth, and from under these heavens:

(Jeremiah 10:10—11)

Jesus answered them, Is it not written in your law, I said, Ye are gods? (referring to Elohim, Psalm 82:6)

If he called them gods (referring to Elohim), *unto whom the word of God came, and the scripture cannot be broken; say ye of him, whom the Father hath sanctified, and sent unto the world, Thou blasphemest; because I said, I am the Son of God?''* (John 10:34—36)

A Scholar's Explanation

Lockyer's "All the Divine Names and Titles of the Bible"* tells us the word Elohim is applied more than 2,300 times to God. It first appears in Genesis 1:1: *In the beginning God (Elohim) created the heaven and the earth.*

Elohim is found in scriptures altogether some 3,000 times and it is through the misuse of this one Hebrew word that opportunity for devilish confusion has resulted. Lockyer tells us of these secondary meanings as shown in the scriptures previously.

In Genesis 3:5 the sense of "gods" is "god-men" — men acting as if they were God. In Psalm 82:6 Lockyer tells us Elohim is "men", and this is quoted in John 10:34—35. In Psalm 8:5 he tells us the meaning is "angels", and that is what we see translated in the Authorised Version. He gives two more usages of Elohim: "idols" as used in Exodus 34:17 and "judges" as used in Exodus 22:8.

* Broad Oak Edition published by Marshall, Morgan and Scott — 1960

"Ye are as Gods" — My own Testimony of Confusion

What an opportunity is presented for those who will pick at Scripture and declare conveniently that Elohim always means God or gods! We hear it taught by many: we are gods but with a little 'g'.

I returned from America with the tape which said "You don't have a god in you; you are one." I was clear in my spirit that this was wrong but when I was challenged by my Christian friend at home who said that the Bible said I was a god, there began a retreat from the truth I had arrived at. What I had received into my spirit the enemy was challenging through my mind, and the solution was, through my will, to get my mind on to the word of God; as it was I didn't really know the scriptures thoroughly enough. As we look at the importance of the mind in the next chapter it will be seen that we are to work out and check out with the Word of God what is received into the spirit.

Alas I didn't do this satisfactorily when I came back from America. Certainly I now looked more fully at the scriptures but I turned also to a mature Christian teacher who was extremely familiar with all the "Faith" and "Positive Confession" teaching and with the scriptures used. Whilst I had absorbed the "Faith" teaching and in that year had attended a week of intensive teaching, for a second time, I hadn't got the revelation — either from God or from the deceiver — for these Elohim scriptures. I hadn't checked out all the teaching as the Bereans did to see whether what was said was true, and I still wasn't doing so effectively. My friend's exposition seemed to be flawless so I accepted I had probably been wrong. After all my favourite faith teacher had always given quotations from Scripture and presumably he knew his Bible better than I! And now there was this clear exposition by one who had helped me personally a great deal, a man with discernment particularly where matters of the New Age were concerned.

At that time I still didn't go back to the set of tapes —
again with plenty of scripture references — from the ''Faith''
teaching meetings I had attended. Had I done so I might have
spotted what incredibly — and given the speed at which the
man talked — I must have missed twice previously. One
reference was to Psalm 8:5 which I have quoted previously.
We were told everywhere else that Elohim was found in the
Old Testament it was translated either as God or as gods in
the King James Version, but the teacher's more startling
statement was that theology in the days of the King James
translators didn't go along with saying that man was on a
level with God after he was born again. I had not seen how
the serpent's lie had infiltrated such a range of Christian
teaching. The Lord had certainly put the need for this book
on my heart, but little had I realised the depth of the deception I would come across in the meantime.

The Truth Dawns

It was not long before the Holy Spirit was prompting me
again. Was I really a god even with a small ''g''? Furthermore even if men were called gods in some scriptures, would
it not be to their discredit and more of a comment on their
misbehaviour? At length, through the scriptures listed earlier,
the truth was revealed to me.

Man wasn't created as a god. God didn't want man to
become as God, but our false aspirations arise through the
disobedience of Adam and Eve. It brought them spiritual
death. Adam had been put in charge of the earth but he was
never god of it. After the fall Satan became the ruler of the
world (1 John 5:19) but that doesn't mean he took the place
of Adam as much teaching today is suggesting.

The false teaching is that it is up to *Man* to take back the
dominion from Satan and once again become the *god* of the
earth. Yet Man never was God of the earth. What Man takes
back is the authority *under God.* Adam was never a god. He
was created to have fellowship with God. It is true that Jesus
was the second Adam, but He came as a man to pay the price

of Man's sins. Jesus is with us and we have the Holy Spirit dwelling in us.

However according to the Bible, and unlike in the all-embracing Hindu view, God is separate from His creation. Fallen Man, through focus on self, acts like a god. That was Adam's position as he left the Garden of Eden. Because of the redemptive work of Jesus, that does not have to be Man's situation today. But when we come to know Jesus as our Saviour and Lord living according to His Word, there is no reason at all to allow ourselves to forget the lesson of the serpent's lie in Genesis 3:5.

Some may rightly say it's no remarkable revelation — to come to the conclusion that men are not to be gods! "Even the world would know that," they might say. They would be correct, and the example points to the danger. It is not an intellectual problem. If it were it would be somewhat easier and those without the Spirit — the world referred to in the above quotation — would have no difficulty with a conclusion reached on that basis. The danger comes in the spiritual realm, and it arises through exposure to such dangerous teaching (the teaching of the very lie of the serpent). How easy it is to forget that we are in a spiritual warfare with a battle that is in the spiritual realm!

Godhood in the New Age

The Antichrist whom the New Age will produce will appear to New Agers as one who has achieved *godhood* through his human potential. They will worship him, and look upon him as one who has developed in a way they too hope to develop. The lie that Man is God and the aspiration to godhood possessed by Man can be expected to hold the Antichrist's organisation together. This can be much the same way as Indian society is held together by the caste system and belief in progressive development based on karma and reincarnation.

I believe there are many potential possible Antichrists in the world today. The spirit of Antichrist is active. Man is encouraged in nearly every area of life to believe his potential comes from within himself, whether it is his psyche, his mind or whatever. Even today the contenders for the role of Antichrist according to Revelation Chapter Thirteen are mightily demon-possessed. The man who will eventually emerge can be expected to display signs and wonders to be evidenced by the whole world on a scale that has not yet been seen. The eventual Antichrist will surely be the last word in human psychic potential. Let us not believe that we are as God according to Scripture, and let us not behave as God in our daily lives. Let us reject the error of the teaching and in that way lend no weight either to the New Age infiltration of the Church or to the New Age Movement outside.

Referring to the proposition, "You don't have a god in you. You are one" Dave Hunt and T.A. McMahon tell us that such statements don't represent slips of the tongue or some new doctrine, but that the idea is at the heart of the Positive Confession Movement today, and can be traced back to numerous groups of earlier eras, such as the Manifest Sons of God and Latter Rain movements. We look at these groups in later chapters. Positive Confession ,*like* signs and wonders, *like* inner healing, *like* shepherding can be scriptural! Indeed it is with our mouth that we confess and are saved (Romans 10:9), and that includes a great deal found in Scripture, but we cannot make a movement or a technique out of any of these things. Our focus has to remain fixed upon Jesus. The alternative is to travel with some in the Positive Confession movement into Possibility Thinking, Positive Thinking and the Positive Mental Attitude movement. Once on that road we soon can find ourselves "believing for" and "confessing" attractive things which our mind suggests to us but which God doesn't want us to have. Rather He has something better when we look only to Him. He has for us more than ever we could ask or think (Ephesians 3:20). Positive Confession is the first of the false teachings examined in detail in Part Two.

I was taken around in a circle until I came right back to the understanding I had gained in America. The interpretation of Elohim had to reckon the context and the whole tenor of Scripture. Jesus didn't only quote to the leaders of His day, *"Ye are gods"* (John 10:34) He also said *"ye are of your father the devil"* (John 8:44). They were behaving as gods without the right to do so. For me the roundabout exercise was a useful one for it focused my attention on scriptures that had for long given comfort to cults like the Mormons. One Christian involved in the "Faith" (Positive Confession) teaching put it to me as the Mormons teach it, namely that Satan told the *truth* when he offered godhood to Eve. However surely such an application of Psalm 82 is unfounded. Verse 6 says *"ye are gods"*. However "gods" is interpreted there, it is in the present tense and not something we *shall* become. Mormons look *forward* to godhood; as we have seen there are Christians who declare we are gods *now*. In a personal letter to me at the time when I was still doubtful of the measure of the error in the "Faith" teaching, Dave Hunt wrote; "It's much worse than you think." Indeed it was.

Satan's blindfold was removed as I prayed earnestly that I might know the truth. I found that the "Faith", "Word" or "Positive Confession" teaching along with other serious errors in the Church was founded on the lie that we are as gods. Indeed I found it could typically lead to still more serious error.

Jesus Said, *"It is not written in your law, I said Ye are gods?"*(John 10:34), but we are not meant to be. The spirit of Antichrist has invaded the Church seeking to flatter believers that we are. Man has always fallen easy prey to pride but in these last days this focus of New Age thinking has come into the Church. Surely the appearance of the Antichrist as beast out of the earth of Revelation 13:11 will seem to many like a second Elijah. We know he will have *"two horns like a **lamb**".* Will he not appear as a committed Christian, as a child of God and very closely resembling the Lord Jesus, the *Lamb* of God? I believe he will. In chapter twelve we look at a group known as the Manifest Sons of God. They may well produce such an outwardly attractive man but he will be a deceiver. We have seen such men already but, perhaps soon, the Antichrist will appear.

Meanwhile we shall see that there are other teachings besides Positive Confession that lead to a focus on godhood and Manifest Sons of God teaching. We shall identify the powerful spirit at work to promote the lie that man was created God of this world and that Satan stole the kingdom from Man. The error is rooted in the idea that we have to take our godhood back from Satan and *establish* the Kingdom, making it possible for Christ to come back and rule over it *when we have established it for Him.* As we shall see, such a false interpretation puts emphasis on the *corporate* body of Christ. We would be Manifest Sons after the pattern of Jesus. He would be the Pattern Son and His rule would be in us. That is the rationale and the "ye are gods" teaching signals that path.

Although few are discerning the direction they are headed, we shall see that the result is to deny the truth that Jesus will return IN THE AIR:

For the Lord himself shall descend from heaven with a shout with the voice of the archangel, and with the trump of God: and the dead in Christ shall rise first:

Then we which are alive and remain shall be caught up together with them in the clouds, to meet the Lord in the air: and so shall we ever be with the Lord.

(1 Thessalonians 4:16—17)

Like the New Agers expecting their "Christ", those believers who are the deceived ones and part of the falling away according to 2 Thessalonians 2:3 will be ready to receive a leader, not in the air but who has his feet ON THE GROUND. He is being promoted now by the spirit of Antichrist in both the Church and the New Age movement alike. The New Agers and deceived Christians already have much in common and will draw closer together as the delusion accumulates through failure to discern the truth. This is preparing the ground for the "strong delusion" (2 Thessalonians 2:11).

The writings of New Age and Church leaders are already

35

extensive. Many do not always seek to conceal their positions. Blatantly apostate interpretations of Scripture, by many who we suppose have received Jesus as Lord and Saviour, are to be found.

Tracing the Root of "Christian" Godhood

Dave Hunt tells us in "The Seduction of Christianity" that it was in the writings of men like E.W. Kenyon, William Branham and John G. Lake that we first find the major "faith" teaching. Thus I was able to trace the root of the tape message that had so astounded me in America: "You don't have a god in you; you are one." I purchased a copy of "The God Men",* a sermon given by Lake and I read how God intended us to be gods. I read of the great awakening that needed to come to all our hearts, that there is a god-power and a soul-force in the nature of man that God is endeavouring to bring forth. I read that as we view the Scripture from beginning to end we see the "wondrous truth" that man is not a separate creation detached from God, but a part of God Himself. I could see this was pantheistic and that Lake was deceived; E.W. Kenyon also.

Soon after becoming a Christian I had bought a copy of "The Blood Covenant" from a visiting preacher. It was written by Kenyon and I well remember the strange enthusiasm with which he praised it, almost to a degree that should be reserved for the Bible. I never read the book until I came to look for what its author had said about our being as gods. I read: "When you learn to walk as Jesus walked, without any consciousness of inferiority to God or Satan, you will have faith that will absolutely stagger the world!"**

---

* "Spiritual Hunger, The God-Men and Other Sermons" by Dr. John G. Lake. Ed. Gordon Lindsay (Christ for the Nations, Dallas — Reprint 1984)
** The Blood Covenant" by E.W. Kenyon (Kenyon's Gospel Publishing Society — 1969, eighteenth edition)

"Christian" Godhood —
Today's Message

I was astounded by the several examples of respected ministries holding to this "ye are gods" teaching. God had got my attention. I began to seek out notes and tapes of various meetings.

One I had attended was a week's course of teaching in Staffordshire given by a powerful though not well-known group of Americans. They came from Tulsa, Oklahoma, a city well known for its output of "Faith" teachers. I had been very impressed by these teachers, also I had heard the tapes afterwards. Now I was listening to the tapes a second time. Was there anything at all about Man being a god? Admittedly there was much on the tapes, spoken at speed and with enthusiasm, but it was only at about the third playing, the fourth time of hearing the message, that I caught what was being said.

The relevant piece centred on the meaning of ELOHIM. Psalm 8:5, we were told, translated it as angels in the King James Version, whereas in every other place in the Old Testament it is translated God or gods. My later study on that, also covered earlier in this chapter, showed this not to be correct. However the result of my enquiry into this very long teaching on "Authority" was to see if there was any reference to Man being a god. I found it.

In that teaching seminar we had been told — and I missed hearing it — that when the King James Version was translated from the original in 1611-1612 the theology of that day didn't go along with saying that Man was on a level with God after he is born again.

The teacher went on to explain that Man was created a god not with a big "G" but with a little "g". Man was created, he said, as god of this world.

This was the lie, sometimes (more often in America) spelled out and sometimes hidden, but nevertheless found to be very evident in a good number of ministries to which

I had been exposed.

Soon afterwards, I was walking up the hill to the church where we attended and I met one of the deacons who knew his Bible well. "Was Adam a god before the fall"? I asked him. "Of course he wasn't," he replied. There I had it, and I came to see in all its simplicity the lie at the root of the so-called "Faith" and "Positive Confession", teaching that I had so enthusiastically followed. This is what the "Faith" people are teaching:

1. Adam was a god.
2. Adam fell and so Satan became god of this world.
3. Jesus, the second Adam, redeemed us by His death and resurrection.
4. Now it is up to us to take back that godhood from Satan.

Such a false view warrants careful comparison to the truth:

1. Adam was given dominion and authority *but under God*.
2. Adam fell and Satan became god of this world.
3. Jesus, the second Adam, redeemed us by His death and resurrection.
4. Now it is up to us to receive Him and get back under God's authority as *redeemed Man*.

However I was to stumble across more and more examples of Christian teachers with messages rooted in the idea that we are gods. We shall meet more examples in later chapters.

The Manifest Sons of God

William Branham, the third of the teachers from the earlier movements quoted by Hunt and McMahon, had a healing ministry that seems to have defied comparison. Because of its extraordinarily suspect nature and the spark Branham gave to the Latter Rain Movement of 1948 which fired the old Manifest Sons of God heresies, we take a close look at the Branham ministry in chapter twelve. His followers believed he was the fulfilment of the prophecy in Malachi 4:5.

Behold I will send you Elijah the prophet before the coming of the great and dreadful day of the Lord:

If this book were to have an alternative title it would be "The Manifest Sons of God" reflecting the focus of Man upon himself, and the doctrine that Christ is not to come in His *physical* body *in the air* but instead is to mysteriously inhabit the Manifest Sons both individually and corporately. The Manifest Sons believe Christ's return will be *in them.*

Another ministry looked at in chapter twelve is Union Life, a magazine outreach closely linked to Manifest Sons teaching. Those exposing the New Age in the Church in America readily acknowledge one contributor's many years of Christian service before accepting the teaching that "ye are gods". However he now believes people are "popping up like mushrooms" here, there and everywhere who are what he calls "knowers", inwardly, by revelation of the Spirit, knowing that they are human forms of Christ — walking about and spontaneously operating in human forms.* There could perhaps be few clearer examples of how Christ is seen as operating in the bodies of believers, not in the sense of the Holy Spirit indwelling Spirit-filled believers, but as "human forms of Christ". Really what we have is men (Manifest Sons) behaving as gods.

The Bible provides for an anointing upon each one of us as believers. In chapter eight we look at "Signs and Wonders", and the readiness of some believers in these days to focus upon them, and upon those who perform them, rather than on Jesus. How tempting it seems to be to confuse Jesus and His anointing with anything we see manifested through men. *"And no marvel; for Satan himself is transformed into an angel of light"* (2 Corinthians 11:14). Surely in these last days the deceptions will go deeper and become more subtle! We shall see later that there are evangelists who tell their audiences: "You are not looking

* see "Union Life" magazine — April 1981

39

at me; you are looking at Jesus." We shall need to beware seeing Christ as an 'anointing'. Eventually there will be one man, exceptionally deceived and exceptionally 'anointed'. He will be the Antichrist manifest in the flesh.

The Holy Spirit dwells in each believer. We can be filled with the Holy Spirit and minister in the name of Jesus, under His anointing, when we give Him the Lordship over our lives. That does not give us licence to act as gods but only and wonderfully to do the will of the Father, walking as Jesus walked, in obedience. The Christian's wonderful expectation is to be with the Lord, in our glorified body like His, when He comes in the air.

The future *on earth* is *not* a rosy one. There is no biblical evidence, nor evidence in the circumstances, to show that things are going to get better. Indeed it is clear from both points of view that they must get worse. Anyone who has looked at the New Age movement cannot be in any doubt. Anyone who reads the newspapers cannot be in any doubt. No one who reads the Bible should be in any doubt.

Ye hypocrites, ye can discern the face of the sky and of the earth; but how is it that ye do not discern this time?
(Luke 12:56)

The truth is that Jesus, the Word, doesn't paint a rosy picture of these last days. We read the truth in 2 Thessalonians 2:9—12 and we are encouraged to test everything and hold fast to that which is good. That is the subject of chapter four.

We need not open ouselves to the ''strong delusion'' and to the serpent's lie. We can test all teaching as the Bereans did in order to see if it is what the Bible says, and we need have no fears since the Holy Spirit will be our interpreter. We can love Jesus, love the truth and so be saved. (2 Thessalonians 2:10)

The common **deception** offered to Christians is that we are ''as gods''. Passivity is the common **cause** of that deception and we look at this in the next chapter.

3

Passivity — The Cause of Much Deception

God has given us sovereign freewill. We are free to choose to be "as gods" or we can choose God's will for our lives. As Christians we have come to know Jesus and we have received the Holy Spirit. Through *Him* we are enabled to keep ourselves filled with the Holy Spirit and we are equipped to hear Him when He quickens our hearts through His Word. As believers we can be transformed by the renewing of our minds (Romans 12:2) and our minds help us with our discernment as we sift what is from God. The powers of darkness of course have quite a different plan. Primarily they influence our minds, but what more can we say about freewill?

Freewill and Obedience

A battle is going on in the spiritual realm, but as Christians we can be dead to self. God's will, not self-will, is our aim. That involves obedience. Through Adam's disobedience we were set to perish, but through Christ's obedience we are saved. More than fifty years ago, Watchman Nee wrote the following, and the picture then was much the same as it is today:

"The purpose of divine salvation is to encourage us to deny our will and be united with Him. Right there lies a big mistake among modern Christians. They envisage spirituality to be a joyous feeling or profound knowledge. They spend

41

time craving various sensations or questing after mental knowledge of the Bible, for they regard these as highly superior. Meanwhile, acting upon their feelings and thoughts, they go about performing many good, grand and notable tasks which they believe must be quite pleasing to God. .... He does not ask the nature of whatever we start; He simply enquires who started it. God discounts every element not yet freed from self, no matter how good it may appear to be.''*

Mind

The powers of darkness are especially prone to attack our minds. In this way they impose their authority. Then through the mind of one they transmit their thoughts to others.

Paul warns the believers in 2 Corinthians 11:4:

For if he that cometh preacheth another Jesus, whom we have not preached, or if ye receive another spirit, which ye have not received, or another gospel, which ye have not accepted, ye might well bear with him.''

How like the Corinthian church is the Church that many of us know today! Watchman Nee saw the peril:

''Satan has disguised himself as an angel of light to lead saints to worship with their intellect a Jesus other than the Lord, to receive a spirit other than the Holy Spirit, and by these to propagate a gospel other than the gospel of the grace of God. Paul pronounces these to be nothing else than the deeds of Satan in the Christian's mind. The adversary translates these 'doctrines' into thoughts and then imposes

---

* ''The Spiritual Man'' (Volume III — page 83) by Watchman Nee (Christian Fellowship Publishers, Inc. New York — 1977 Edition. Available from Christian Fellowship Publishers, Inc., 11515 Allecingle Parkway, Richmond, Virginia 23235, USA)

The book was written more than fifty years ago and translated into English only after Nee's death. In the context of this quotation Nee writes of God seeking a ''union'' of our own wills with His will. Some scholars have understandably cautioned against the misinterpretation of a sort of mysticism. While not seeking here to endorse all of Nee's writing in this way, the author, himself totally rejecting pantheism (the doctrine that God is everything and everything God, much favoured in China and the East where Nee came from), believes ''The Spiritual Man'' was written with that same understanding. We have freewill to be obedient to God's will.

them upon the mind of the Christian. How tragic that few appreciate the reality of these activities! Few indeed who would ever think that the devil could give such thoughts to men! It is possible for a child of God to have a new life and new heart but be without a new head. With too many saints, the mind, though their heart is new, is still quite old. Their heart is full of love whereas their head is totally lacking in perception.''*

My own book is addressed humbly to the sincere men of our own day, to the godly men, to many who have behind them lives of service with which my own efforts could never be compared, to men who are fully committed to the Lord. I write for the many whose hearts are wonderfully full of love, yet whose heads are lacking in perception.

Satan seeks to bring wrong doctrine to the Christian mind. It is true, as Watchman Nee also writes, that *life* is a thousand times more important than knowledge. The Christian is saved and he has *life,* but next after salvation has to come the transformation of our minds. Paul tells us we are now not to conform any longer to the pattern of this world, *"But be ye transformed by the renewing of your mind."* (Romans 12:2).

It takes effort to bring renewal to our minds when we have become Christians. Even as we seek to leave our worldly ways behind the enemy will be out to tempt us back. We do have sovereign control of our own will. We do have a choice of what we receive into our minds and as Christians we can know God's way. Through His Word and the prompting of the Holy Spirit we can know what is His will for us. He wills that we are transformed by the renewal of our minds.

I did not find it easy to make my mental processes subject to my will, but real progress could be made when I understood Satan's tactics from Scripture.

Intuition where Christians are concerned needs to come from the Holy Spirit. Guidance from the Holy Spirit bringing

* ''The Spiritual Man'' (Volume III — page 11)

a focus on Jesus and the Word is essential and peculiar to the Christian life. It is to be the basis on which our will is to work in harmony with God. It is to be the basis for the action we take. Also before we get to exercising that freewill, our minds can be renewed through submission to God's will and His word, and not debilitated by the invasion of the enemy. It is with our enlightened minds that we are able to check out whether an idea is from God. Such discernment comes through minds enlightened by and attuned to the Holy Spirit and the Word of God, through minds uncluttered by the confusion of thoughts we had never *intended* to think.

We need our minds also in order to put into effect what we have heard the Holy Spirit say to us. If we have heard Him correctly then it can surely be possible, through God's grace, that our minds (and our bodies) will cope with whatever we have to do. But we need to keep our enlightened minds active. We have to beware the state of passivity, a state of neglected mind that is all too seldom fully recognised in these days where emphasis is so often not on Jesus who is the Word.

The significance of our minds is well understood by Satan. As we shall see it is all too easy, as Christians, to neglect the mind without realising it.

Neglected Minds Open to Lies

Some will not hear what the Holy Spirit is saying and they will not read their Bibles. They may well fall at the point of Genesis 3:5 believing, like Eve, that they too can be "as gods". They will believe this very basic lie, sadly the underlying message of many Christian ministries in these days.

As Christians we are to die to self, but so far is the lie of the serpent advanced that there is even another gospel known as the Gospel of Self-Esteem. This is a gospel that is infiltrating Christian thinking worldwide and it is being powerfully promoted through TV (in America) and through evangelism which focuses on prosperity and the power of positive thinking.

Along a similar road, without regard for the principle of Scripture that it must be read in the context of what the writer was saying and balanced up with the whole message of the Bible, many sail along on an intellectual understanding — a limited one at that — after falling for the deceptive doctrine of ''Name It and Claim It.''

Satan works through the mind of a Karate exponent. Such men have been persuaded as to a lie and they will be used to persuade others. They are persuaded that their minds can overcome matter. Asked how it is done, they will say ''mind over matter''. On TV I saw two karate experts who were demolishing a brick-built house (in half a day) with their bare hands. The message is that mind can overcome matter. As Christians, if we are sick in our bodies or in our emotions we may find ourselves tempted in the direction of what are really mind-centred ideas with Christian labels. Many of these techniques are disguised under the all-embracing label of Inner Healing. As in Karate, though I don't draw the parallel any closer than this, it isn't the mind that gets the results; the healing agent is the demon power that is at work.

I believe there is an element of mind-power involved with many healing techniques and so-called alternative therapies, just as there is in many areas of the occult. We look at homoeopathy in particular in chapter nine, but, as we shall see, mind-power is neither Satan's only ingredient in altern-ative medicine nor in his strategy for the infiltration of the Church.

Another area for concern at this time is the unbalanced focus on just 'signs and wonders'. As any medical doctor knows, a big proportion of patients lose their symptoms by methods which feed their minds. They are given placebos, and placebo means ''to please''. The placebo may be nothing more than an inert preparation coated with coloured sugar. However it pleases the patient and it does the trick. Often the placebo isn't inert, for how can a doctor justify such an inert or inactive method to his patient? So next there are the side-effects of some other active but unnecessary pill. Against this shallow treatment, the genuine healing of God goes deep, and there need be no mistaking a miracle when it comes from Him. How different from that are many of the 'signs and wonders' that capture the minds and imaginations of Christians today!

It is true that God is at work; it is true that Jesus is the Healer. But how close does much of the ministry come to that of the placebo? And what are the consequences where there is no discernment and the deceiver has a foothold in a "signs and wonders" ministry? They are worse than the usual side effects of a placebo, but we have for long focused on getting rid of our pains and our problems, going to men for their solution, that it becomes difficult to address the question: "Which power is at work?" It is imperative that we don't receive our healing from demons. We return to "signs and wonders" in chapter eight but a first step is to realise that demons can get their way through our minds.

Believers join their churches and fellowships for prayer and to praise and worship God. This can properly take many forms that need not be mentioned here. However demons seek to bring deception both to the body of believers and wherever pastor and people minister one to another.

In spiritual groups we find silence and meditation; we find chanting and singing. Without discernment the end result of this can be the passivity found in cult gatherings and among people moving in the occult realm.

Music

Music is very significant in the New Age. There are types of music which will quickly induce a state of passivity. Alice Bailey, whose occult writings I describe in "Understanding the New Age", taught what we are seeing today. Music Therapy was in her view a significant item to prepare the world for the New Age. We have seen the relevance of Rock, including the worst heavy metal sounds, on the secular scene. Its infiltration of the Church, long since begun, has now settled to a state of respectability with its worst excesses readily accepted by more and more Christians slowly blinded and deluded. My own experience of the "Greenbelt" Festival lasts in my memory. Yet this flagship for the Christian pop world has given the idea to less outrageous ventures. With the seed planted, the rest can become more outrageous too. In God's purpose there is no place for such mixture. Except the error be driven out, the mixture will become more polluted.

"Stryper are here! The long awaited, much anticipated band that's set to revolutionise contemporary Christian music are the album of the month .... with their latest release 'To Hell with the Devil'." So began the letter from Record Club Editor, Kate Tattum to her readers in 1987.

Who then are Stryper? They are a "heavy metal" band. According to the Word Record Club Magazine, the group takes its name and visual image from Isaiah 53 ("By His stripes ..."). "Stryper have shaken the foundations wherever they've been heard .... they launched their all-out assault on American ears with a blinding stage show and a first album on the same label as the self-avowedly repulsive Motley Crue. That album became the biggest-selling independent LP of the year in the USA .... But for an unfortunate booking mix-up, Stryper would have headed the Greenbelt '86 bill."*

The leaders of our Christian youth, from the grass roots to the highest national levels in Christian leadership, have an urgent need to discern the damage that is being caused by the world's music. At the root of the problem is the need to understand the dangers of passivity and its relevance in introducing minds to the occult realm. Given a high noise level or the right beat, the mind will "switch off" and become passive.

Passivity in the Occult Realm

Experiences can follow minds which are away from God,

* "Word Record Club Magazine" (Word (UK) Ltd — 1987)

47

not focused on His word and not attuned to the Holy Spirit; passive minds are open to experiences. As it is never God who brings passivity, how can we expect that the resulting experiences will be from Him?

In the occult realm the spiritualist or meditator looks forward to receiving a clairvoyant, clairaudient or "healing" gift. As Christians we know these are counterfeit abilities. The experiences of some include astral travel where the meditator is aware of being outside of his physical body. Others can take hold of a pen and allow the spirits full contol to perform "automatic writing" quite independently of the mind of the one who is deceived. Whether it is any of these things, or even a witch sticking a pin in an effigy and expecting the death of his tribal enemy (or a witch doctor who brings "healing" or the removal of a curse from a patient), the power is satanic.

Others are able to "visualise". A powerful witch may not need an effigy. It can be sufficient in one so taken over by demons that he or she simply visualises what the powers of darkness intend to bring about. The powers who bring about these abominable deeds are equipped, in the way of the witch *doctor,* to bring relief also.

In the West today, and more and more in the churches, there are those who now exercise mind power. They visualise their subjects in a state of good health. Like the God they counterfeit, demons have no strict categorisation of methods. They will even use the name of Jesus if it suits the purpose of deception, and Christians and non-Christians alike can be brought to a place where they can visualise Jesus. But it will be another 'Jesus' and not the one believers know. There is no scriptural warrant for a visualised Jesus; we walk with Him by faith. This may be one of God's reasons why He is not described other than in Isaiah's prophecies.

Passivity is not to suggest only silence or inactivity. The mark of a successful yogi is that he can maintain the "switched off", peaceful state even when he gets up from his strange body positions. His mind succeeds over matter so enabling him to achieve supernatural feats not given to

48

most.

Christians or professing Christians who innocently fall into Hindu, New Age, and occultic methods will find that they work. Yet the price to pay, whether physically, mentally or spiritually will sooner or later be a high one. The need especially in these end days is for believers to believe they *can* be deceived. That is not a matter of negative confession or a negative faith. It is clear from Scripture and plain common sense. The disciples were themselves so passive in their great time of temptation that they went to sleep (Matthew 26:40) but Peter was later to warn us (1 Peter 5:8) that if we become passive and intemperate the devil will devour us. The need is to be "sober and vigilant".

Moral Re-Armament (MRA) — The danger of the "Quiet Time"

From the beginning of my time as a "searcher" in the realm of the cults and the occult I knew a peace. It wasn't that peace that the world gives; rather it was a somewhat closer counterfeit of the peace which we know "passes all understanding". That peace remained as I reunited myself with the cult of Moral Re-Armament (MRA) after about twenty years. Referring to Watchman Nee's writings yet again, as a Christian I was able to relate my own experience of MRA to what I have known in some Christian groups. In a section named "Joy and Peace" Watchman Nee shows just how easy it is to obtain this so-called peace and he refers to the "Quiet Time" known in MRA:

"What is the highest attainment in Christianity? That of complete union with God and total loss of self. In modern psychology there is also the so-called union of man with the invisible "mind" so as to cause him to lose his identity. This appears to be akin to Christianity, though in reality these two are far apart. The popular Dr. Frank Buchman (Oxford Group movement) (Author's Note: The Oxford Group later became MRA) advocated this kind of psychology. One of

49

his teachings concerned meditation. He reckoned that meditation was all that was necessary for communication between man and God. He did not ask people to read the Bible at early morn; he only asked them to meditate and then to pray. The first thought which comes after prayer, he proclaimed, is that thought which is given you by God. And so you must live through the day according to that thought. Who would ever think that this is but another type of silent sitting or abstract meditation? You will be told that it will make you most peaceful and joyous. If you quietly direct your thought on whatever thing it may be for an hour, you too will get what is called peace and joy. Even if you meditate abstractly for one hour on no thought at all, you will still not fail to obtain this so-called peace and joy. The meditations of many people are simply a kind of psychic operation. Not so with Christian faith .... we have the word of God. Whatever His word says, we believe. If we have faith, we can disregard feeling. Herein lie the differences between Christian faith and psychology.''*

Certainly God gives us a peace and many know God's peace today, but let us note this influence of the Frank Buchman teaching because the significance of this philosophy is more and more recognisable in parts of the charismatic movement today. I believe that some who say they "feel a peace", about this or about that, have the same peace that Buchman, himself a born-again believer, knew.

With this background of MRA, a cult including some believers but now centred far away from Christ, I have been aware in some measure of the dangers. From that time in MRA my path led into occult meditation and healing. It is against that experience, whilst endeavouring to be both cautious and fairminded in the light of God's word, that I have been alerted.

* ''The Spiritual Man''

50

Biblical Camouflage for a Passive Mind

I have been alerted to the similarities and dangers evident in at least some of the charismatic and pentecostal groups that I have visited. There can be biblical camouflage for the passive mind. Prophecy is perhaps the gift where the results lend themselves most readily to analysis. If I had made a note of all the prophecies I heard spoken in the past five years since becoming a Christian, it would be an extraordinary list. How many others have heard that a friend would be healed; and yet he died? How many have heard that *their* church or *their* town was to be the centre of revival? It is no wonder there can be many examples when it is a common teaching that we have to "practise" using the gift. At one large conference a well-known charismatic teacher was encouraging even young children, grouped into pairs, to prophesy one to another. Satan can achieve much in damaging God's church through such sincere and so-called spiritually advanced leaders working with believers, children or adults, who have passive and unquestioning minds.

This passivity requires good explanation because, in its various forms, it is at the heart of what we find in the occult; more significantly here, we say again that it is all too often the order of the day in those churches which seek after the gifts and the experiences whilst neglecting solid teaching from the word of God.

Becoming full of the Word is the way that the Word itself teaches. On the other hand we find those who neglect it are, on the basis of a quiet meditation, all too ready to accept the thoughts they receive as being those of God. A well-known teacher makes the point for us in the following quotation:

"The prayer for guidance begins with a period of waiting. You come before the Lord, and you just get quiet. There is no activity, but rather a passivity. You are trying to hear .... You even quit breathing so you can hear better."*

That is but one of the many ways to passivity. In the church

* "The Christian Family" by Larry Christenson (Bethany Fellowship, Inc. Minneapolis, Minnesota) — 1970

setting we see pastors preparing the ground at the start of the meetings, getting the mood right. Various emotional and worldly ways can be used. We find rhythm, beat, clapping and noise. The wrong spirit is easily spread; young Christians and visitors from dead churches can be easily impressed by caring people and lively meetings. Self- effort and emotion is all to easily confused with the work of the Holy Spirit.

The early or eventual result of all this is a passivity — a deadness of spirit and a Christian variation of what happens to the kids in the disco. Passivity can be the result of a "praise time" just as it can result from a "quiet time". In a similar fashion the disco with all its noise and flashing lights induces a passivity just as effectively as the "quiet time" known in MRA or the strobe lighting and meditation which, as a "searcher" I indulged in in the quiet of my office.

The whole point of emphasising what we have called passivity, and of making comparisons with cultic and occultic practices, becomes clearer when we understand the devil and his ways. The Bible says *"My people are destroyed for lack of knowledge ...."* (Hosea 4:6) and yet there is seen in the Church generally a marked lack of knowledge of the conditions which set demons to work. There is a widespread failure to understand that the principles are the same whether these conditions are deliberately established (as with a witch or a medium) or whether they are met in innocence by the Christian with good motives. In "The Spiritual Man" Watchman Nee draws the comparison to the fire that scorches or the water that drowns: "It pays no heed to whether one is a Christian or not; once the conditions are met, the evil spirits do not fail to act."

Some fifty odd years ago Watchman Nee wrote that a main reason for deception in surrendered believers — and my book is written mainly with these in mind — was passivity, a cessation of the active exercise of the will over the spirit, soul and body. Jesse Penn Lewis,* along with Watchman Nee, but unlike so many believers then and now saw passivity as:

* "War on the Saints" by Jesse Penn Lewis

1. Loss of self-control — in the sense of the person himself controlling all of his personal being, and
2. Loss of freewill — in the sense of the person himself exercising his will "as the guiding principle of personal control", in harmony with the will of God.

When I was saved it was my mistake that for a time I lapsed into a state of not questioning things I was asked or told by those in authority in the fellowship where I became a member. I used to reason that if the leaders said it and I did it then God would honour it! I used to think that much that happened in my life and circumstances was from God, but really it was easier to be driven along by circumstances than to exercise freewill in a proper way.

In "The Spiritual Man" there is painted a scenario that is common among those who do not see freewill as God sees it: "He seems to be happy when forced to do anything, for this keeps him from anxiety which would arise from indecision. He would rather be driven by circumstances since making a choice is so trying for him. In such a condition of inertia, to decide a small matter becomes a tremendous chore! The victim looks for help everywhere. He feels quite embarrassed because he does not know how to cope with his daily affairs. He seems hardly to understand what people say to him. Painful it is for him to recall anything; agonising it is to make a decision; terrifying, to consider any task. His inert will is impotent to bear such a heavy responsibility. Because of its gross weakness he is compelled to wait for assistance through environment or through men .... In his foolishness the Christian does not perceive that all these symptoms flow from passivity and invasion but instead believes they are merely his natural weaknesses .... Know that these are caused by the evil spirits whether one perceives it or not. Being well acquainted with the believer's current condition, the powers of darkness will foment many troubles in his environment to disturb him .... The powers of darkness have gained the upper hand, all because their victim has fallen from ignorance to deception, from deception to passivity and from passivity to deep entrenchment."

There we see the position of many who are being constantly "ministered to" in the body of Christ today: then to add to the problem some of the church leaders are themselves deceived, passive, and entrenched where false spirits have set them. As regards these unfortunate leaders Nee wrote that we must not make the mistake of believing that those believers who are deceived by evil spirits are also the most defiled, degenerate and sinful. On the contrary, he tells us, they are often "fully surrendered Christians, spiritually more advanced than ordinary believers."* The result of this in my own observation can be leaders burdened by the needs of the people they see around them. They then look here there and everywhere for ways to help. The result is the departure from Scripture, the excesses and the New Age infiltration of the church. We seek to identify some of this infiltration in these pages in order that Christians might be helped in their discernment of it.

Those Christians who have failed to grasp that they have sovereign control over their own will are the ones who all too readily put themselves into the hands of counsellors, who they often don't know, first one then another. They go to meeting after meeting, conference after conference. We can read in "The Spiritual Man" of the consequences that can await Christians who reach this position:

"When the Christian has sunk into such a state he unconsciously may even rely upon the help of evil spirits. He cannot will anything by himself, hence looks for outside forces to help him. He is troubled often by evil spirits, yet he innocently expects these same spirits to come to his aid. This is the reason why they desire to make him passive .... They delight in enticing a person to follow outside revelation blindly without using either thought or will; they therefore often impart a host of strange and supernatural phenomena to men. The Christian, unaware of the principle of God's working, assumes he is being obedient to God when actually he is a prey to deception. Let us be advised of this

* "The Spiritual Man"

54

verse in Romans 6: *'Do you not know that if you yield yourselves to anyone as obedient slaves, you are slaves of the one whom you obey ....?'* (verse 16)"*

God does not want us through our passivity to yield ourselves to demons as obedient slaves. God requires us to have fellowship actively with Him. He requires that we spend time with Him and in His word. God requires that we be taught, yet that we check out the teaching as the Bereans did. That is the way to avoid passivity and to keep the will in control over spirit, soul and body.

To be passive is in effect to abandon or "switch off". This is not the "self-control" described by Paul in the fruit of the Spirit (Galatians 5:23 NIV); it is the opposite. The yogis switch off wherever they are, staring into the fire or going about their business. Westerners are meditating and staring into their strobe lights. Our children (those of the world and all those in the "Christian" discos) are switching off with the help of the beat, the noise, the rhythm and the lights. The world can be an alarming place; every kind of passivity seems to afford relief. The price is a high one.

When the world sees a yogi or meditating New Ager emerge to protest at some military base, it sees a people of peace. Yet it is a peace that the world and the deceiving spirits have given to them. They have become the victims of passivity. Drugs of course have helped many on this road.

Surely the more the Church seeks to attract the world by being like it, and as we have seen in the case of rock music the greater are the risks it faces, sadly what we see is a body that is more like the world than it realises. I have attended services that resembled a disco!

While we are considering passivity it is interesting to make a further point when comparing "lively" and "dead" churches and when comparing believers and unbelievers. Ground is given to demons through sin. James 4:17 speaks of our *failure* to exercise our will: *"Therefore to him that knoweth to do good, and doeth it not, to him it is sin."*

* "The Spiritual Man"

55

Passivity is a sin of omission.

As believers we are not without other sins too, but passivity is the subtle way of deception for the spiritually advanced. Those who fail to take spiritual things seriously do not really face this danger. Once again we trace back to the sovereign will of man to find the clue. Even in the present day reawakening to spiritual things on the occult and on the Christian front, we find nothing like a preponderance of people who run the slightest risk of being accused of falling into passivity! Within this vast majority will be included some who are professing consecration to God, but even they are living on their own ideas and a powerful selfwill prevails.

Again Nee's description fits many today, pastors and people alike: "Only those committed ones who disregard their own interests are open to passivity. Their will can easily slip into this state since they are most eager to obey all orders."*

It's to those committed ones that this book is addressed. The line of divide from those who are following deceiving spirits is so easily crossed where there is a lack of spiritual discernment. We shall see a much healthier church when pastors and people are encouraged in their ministries by receiving this discernment and knowing just *which* orders they are to obey.

Testing the Spirits

Beloved, believe not every spirit, but try the spirits whether they are of God: because many false prophets are gone out into the world. (1 John 4:1)

Watchman Nee paints another scene that is still relevant today:

"Should one's mind be passive, it will be easy for the enemy to inject nonsensical notions in to him, for instance telling him: 'You are God's special vessel' or 'Your work will shake the whole world' or 'you are much more spiritual

* "The Spiritual Man"

than the rest' or 'You should take another course' or 'God will soon open up a wide door for your preaching' or 'You should step out to live by faith' or 'Your spiritual usefulness is unlimited'. Heady thoughts like these disarm all the vigilance of the saint. He thrives day and night on these ideas — dreaming how great and marvellous he is. Not employing the rationalism of his mind, he fails to realise how harmful and how laughable these notions can be in his spiritual walk. He indulges in them by continuously imagining how glorious his future is going to be. Some who deliver messages for the Lord are often governed by these bursting thoughts. They preach what has been revealed to them suddenly. They construe their sudden thoughts to be from God and so accept them passively. They do not understand that God neither gives sudden revelation nor imparts it to the mind."*

That's all very well, some will say, but how do we test the spirits! I believe the priority is to come back to learning from the Word of God. The Holy Spirit quickens it to us. The Holy Spirit speaks to our hearts. Secondly believers need to admit to themselves and to God that they could be wrong, and indeed that they could have been wrong for a very long time. They need to admit that they could be hearing a great deal from evil spirits. As we consider the support Christians give for the deceptive teachings described in the later chapters of this book, then it must be the case that there is a mighty deception. Indeed our Bible tells us:

Now the Spirit speaketh expressly, that in the latter times some shall depart from the faith, giving heed to seducing spirits, and doctrines of devils; (1 Timothy 4:1).

Through the Holy Spirit we can know His will for us. We can understand it and work it out with our minds; freely exercising our will we can do it. Such is the alternative to the way of passivity. God does not compel action and there is no bypassing the mind's processes.

* ''The Spiritual Man'' (Volume II — page 31)

4

Test Everything : Hold on to the Good

Immediately before receiving Jesus as my personal Saviour and Lord I had been occupied on a full-time basis as a "searcher" in the occult realm of the spiritual dimension. I discovered this dimension only after forty-four years of life. Twenty years of church-going abandoned some fifteen years earlier had not given the key to any sort of spiritual break-through. When the reality of the supernatural world did dawn I did not know that what I had discovered was the occult realm. Occult means hidden. According to the Bible this is Satan's kingdom, and it should have stayed hidden.

Nevertheless I pressed on and made discoveries. I was searching, along with so many in these days, for the truth. The search was in the wrong place but at length I found Jesus in whom I had been chosen from the beginning (Ephesians 1:3—4). After what seemed a remarkable conversion I believed I had found the truth at last. Certainly I recognised the counterfeit power at work in the healing, divination and all of the occult areas I had been involved with, but at first I didn't reckon that my search for the truth would need to continue. On the contrary I now find that there is such depth to the Word of God that it will be never ending.

The need to discern the counterfeit, also in the Body of Christ itself, was brought home to me when I found little understanding in the Church of just where I had come from and how close to the pit I had been. There was little grasp of the dangers of Satan's subtle methods of healing and altern-ative medicine, and the Lord soon put it on my heart to write about it.

As I became more knowledgeable in Scripture and recognised the need to check out all teaching against Scripture (Acts 17:11), I could see that there was much that was not right in the Church. Alternative medicine and healing by those having little or no discernment was part of the New Age. There was in fact a New Age Movement. I realised this was the counterfeit bride Satan was preparing just as Jesus was building His Church. This New Age had overspilled into the Church.

Charismatic "Mixture"

Having been saved in a Pentecostal church, the Lord immediately began to strip me of my occultic connections, then my involvement in the New Age.

In the first two years as a Christian, still full-time, reading, listening to tapes, looking in on the church scene in Europe and America, attending courses and conferences, I saw many who were having experiences of many kinds. I saw the Lord was doing a work wherever I went — souls were being saved. I was impressed and I earnestly sought after the gifts that were manifest in my own church and elsewhere, all within the charismatic movement.

Certainly Christ was being preached; that was the important thing:

"What then? notwithstanding, every way, whether in pretence, or in truth, Christ is preached; and I therein do rejoice yea, and will rejoice" (Philippians 1:18)

After about two years I was discerning a "mixture"; not all in the body of Christ was of God!

During these first two years I made my first visit to the United States as a Christian and spent the entire four weeks, in between a big schedule of speaking engagements, learning about the Christian scene in America. The charismatic scene is somewhat exaggerated in the United States compared to what we know in Britain. This makes discernment easier, and also I became alert to the New Age

60

movement. I had really been a part of it without knowing the name, but through the Lord's leading at that time and the greater awareness they have in America I came to understand how the New Age had touched my life more than I had realised. It took two further years, including the second visit to America described in chapter one, before I could very well understand the depth of the infiltration by the enemy and the extent of the "mixture" to be found in the Church. This book is the result.

I sought and prayed for more experiences than ever came forth through my own ministry as a new Christian. Indeed my "experiences" were minimal, for which I praise God. Thus my testimony is what I *experienced* in the occult realm; then mostly to what I *observed* of the charismatic "mixture" as a Christian. For this reason I quote the testimony of an evangelist, Alexander Seibel. He refers to the warnings, the same warnings now sounded in this book:

"There was a time in my Christian life when I esteemed all these warnings lightly and reached out after these experiences and gifts with all my heart …. Joy, power, wonderful "spiritual" experiences, more prayer and inner certainty, were simply so overpowering and beautiful that there could be no doubt that this was from God. Only after months did I realise my dependence on spiritual experiences and feelings. Yet these doubts were driven back again by the 'evidence' of the positive success in the beginning, for people had even been saved.

…. Anyone who thinks the working of evil spirits has to be always negative outwardly is greatly mistaken.

At the beginning, just for the sake of winning our confidence, the enemy works an imitation of God's presence in us and thus produces the most positive effects and results. Anyhow, my dependency on the feeling of a spiritual high grew. Looking back I can only say that I literally fulfilled those principles of passivity of which God's word warns us. I could let myself passively glide in prayer for hours. I felt myself carried away by an invisible power. It was a pleasant floating feeling. I only had to close my eyes and

61

open myself to this inner force. If I pressed my hands against my face the feeling of this inward floating would become distinctly stronger. Besides, this is a typical spiritistic symptom. Here we find that power is mediated through hands. Sometimes I could meditate in this inner state of passivity for hours. Many suggestions for prayer which I have found in certain literature — and such suggestions and books are increasing steadily — are exactly in accord with these phenomena. The believer thinks because he is a child of God this spiritual reality and experience must unquestionably come from the Holy Spirit. This is how I thought — at least for some time. After such meditations and ''quiet times'' I was often enormously happy, enthusiastic, simply blessed. One really depends on these experiences. Today I know that what I practised had more resemblence to transcendental meditation than to biblical prayer. But I did not realise this at that time. This is how badly blinded I was: the Lord needed more than a year — thanks be to Him for His unfathomable patience and love — before He could open my eyes to this cunning snare of Satan. Only after I repented was I allowed to see the truth (2 Timothy 2:26). It is almost an unbelievable deception.

However, today I understand much better the reason why our Lord Jesus admonishes us in the Lord's Prayer to pray that we may be delivered from evil (Matthew 6:13). I believe that anyone who has not experienced this deception 'in their own body' and had his eyes opened through God's grace can hardly form an idea of how subtle this deception really is. Since then, my counselling experiences have proved dozens of times, sometimes in an amazingly impressive way, the deceptions and the deceit of believers, especially in the charismatic field. If I had not experienced it so clearly in the case of God's children, and had I not been confronted with these manifestations I would not be able to warn of these things so distinctly, or try to speak in such a decisive way. I would like to cry out with all my heart:

'Please let yourselves be warned. We are dealing with

a wave of deception of the worst degree.' ''*

We are dealing with deception of a very high degree. Are we dealing with the ''strong delusion''?: (2 Thessalonians 2:11) about which Paul writes. Is the New Age ''mixture'' in the body of believers getting stronger day by day?

''Balance'' — Needed in the Church!

While Watchman Nee, Alexander Seibel and other watchmen — we can all be watchmen — shout ''Fire'', the blind shout back ''Balance! Balance! Keep your Balance.''

All around me in the Body of Christ was an air of expectancy of Church growth, revival and the manifestation of ever more signs and wonders. There was talk of prosperity and teaching which majored on this being God's will for us. I found the occult in Inner Healing ministries and little understanding of the difference between God's way and Man's way, often through psychology. Certainly God appeared to be moving in a new way; He had just transformed me and given me new life. He was doing that week by week. I was seeing God at work all around me and I was feeding on His Word. Yet it seemed there would be a trumpet I would have to sound. Soon I was taken to 2 Thessalonians 2 having marked carefully Paul's words in 1 Thessalonians 4:17. At the obvious risk of being labelled a ''gloom and doomer'' (and I have been!) it was clear that balance was needed in the Church. *I* would be accused of being out-of-balance by bringing it, but the purpose was that *balance* be brought to the *Church*. When I first read 1 Thessalonians 4:17 in the context of the warning against Antichrist in 2 Thessalonians 2, I didn't realise that this *one* verse would be the one Satan would especially seek to present wrongly. We have seen in the previous chapter how it is a principal message of this book that the focus of much of the error involves the lie that man will establish the Kingdom with God coming, not *in the air* but to live *in us*. The Restoration

* ''The Church Infiltrated'' by Alexander Seibel (B.B.C., Printers and Publishers, Secunderabad, India — translated from the German — 1984)

of the Kingdom would thus be Man's achievement, and rule would be through those who make it as Manifest Sons after the pattern of Jesus. That is the wrong interpretation of Scripture. 1 Thessalonians 4:17 states:

Then we which are alive and remain shall be caught up together with them in the clouds, to meet the Lord in the air; and so shall we ever be with the Lord.

How important that scripture is! It speaks of the day we look forward to as Christians, and surely even more so in this generation. It describes the return of Jesus and the day we shall be caught up at the trumpet call of God with the dead in Christ who have risen first (1 Thessalonians 4:16) in order to be with Him.

Rapture or Wrath?

We are to encourage one another with words of the Lord's return *in the air* (1 Thessalonians 4:18). That is a different event from His return to rule and reign. Paul then goes on to write about *"the day of the Lord"* (5:2), the wrath, trouble and distress that will come *"as a thief in the night"* This will bring a *"sudden destruction"* to a people who are saying *"peace and safety"*. Then Paul further encouraged them:

For God hath not appointed us to wrath, but to obtain salvation by our Lord Jesus Christ

(1 Thessalonians 5:9)

In 2 Thessalonians 2:2 Paul writes that *"the day of the Lord"* has not already come, and that it will not come until there is a *"falling away"*, in a doctrinal sense, and until the *"man of sin"* appears. Whether we believe in a pre- or post-Tribulation rapture of the saints according to 1 Thessalonians 4:17, it is clear we can receive the message as the Thessalonians were to receive it. We are not yet in the period of the wrath or Tribulation, for whilst the falling away is quite certainly in process, the man of sin, the Antichrist of Revelation 13, has not yet been revealed.

Godly scholars interpret these Thessalonian scriptures in

different ways, and the above scriptures from the Second Epistle may describe the situation after the Church is taken out of the world. In this case, and supported particularly by 2 Thessalonians 1:10, what we see in chapter two is for the most part a description of what happens after *"he shall come to be glorified in his saints.... "*

Now we beseech you, brethren, by the coming of our Lord Jesus Christ, and by our gathering together unto him,

That ye be not soon shaken in mind, or be troubled, neither by spirit nor by word, nor by letter as from us, as that the day of Christ is at hand.

Let no man deceive you by any means: for that day shall not come, except there come a falling away first, and that man of sin be revealed, the son of perdition;

Who opposeth and exalteth himself above all that is called God, or that is worshipped; so that he as God sitteth in the temple of God, shewing himself that he is God.

Remember ye not, that, when I was yet with you, I told you these things?

And now ye know what withholdeth that he might be revealed in his time.

For the mystery of iniquity doth already work: only he who now letteth will let, until he be taken out of the way.

And then shall that Wicked be revealed, whom the Lord shall consume with the spirit of his mouth, and shall destroy with the brightness of his coming:

Even him, whose coming is after the working of Satan with all power and signs and lying wonders,

And with all deceivableness of unrighteousness in them that perish; because they received not the love of the truth, that they might be saved.

*And for this cause God shall send them strong **delusion**, that they should believe a lie:*

*That they might be dammed who believed not the **truth**, but had pleasure in unrighteousness.*

(2 Thessalonians 2:1—12)

I believe that the errors in the Church highlighted in this book are significant parts of the *delusion.* Jesus Himself spoke of these days:

And Jesus answered and said unto them, Take heed that no man deceive you.

For many shall come in my name, saying, I am Christ; and shall deceive many ....

And many false prophets shall rise, and shall deceive many ....

For there shall arise false Christs, and false prophets, and shall shew great signs and wonders; insomuch that, if it were possible, they shall deceive the very elect.''

(Matthew 24:4,5,11,24)

Whether we apply these verses to the situation today or to the Kingdom in which the Lord will rule glorified in His saints, what I believe we can say is that the ''strong delusion'' referred to will captivate those who have refused to love the truth, and it is the preparation for that which we are surely seeing today. What we are seeing, and what will be described later is the staging of the Antichrist, the New Age ''Messiah''.

So how then can we know when there are deceiving spirits at work in the Body of Christ? A love of the truth and a good knowledge of the Word is obviously helpful, but what is greatly lacking in the Church is a sharp *discernment* both of doctrine and those who teach it. Today ''big-name'' Christian Bible teachers, sincere and innocently stepping into the web of deception, are actually speaking the words ''I am Christ''. When the deception is not even subtle, and yet still it succeeds, surely this is a sign that the times are near their end. The apostle John cautions us to test every spirit: thus the Lord will make it possible for each one of us to do that.

Beloved, believe not every spirit, but try the spirits whether they are of God: because many false prophets are gone out into the world. (1 John 4:1)

The discernment comes from God, and with it there will come a healthy and fearless scepticism of any new revelation said to come from God. Given a godly jealousy for the truth, the false can be exposed, uprooted and forced out into the open. Knowledge, discernment and experience will make this possible. Let us risk being wrongly described as negative; we recognise that we are in a battle that has to be fought against the error Satan will, ever more subtly, bring our way. Natural reasoning and intuition are not enough and those using the gift of discernment are really bound to encounter opposition from the many who are not.

Discernment

Understandably, like intuition, discernment is difficult to explain. This book is one attempt to explain and encourage it, yet it is a supernatural gift of the Holy Spirit. It is not necessarily rational or logical. It must be in step with Scripture. Discernment is the means the Holy Spirit uses to show us what is of God and what is not. Very few attempt a definition and it could even be said that it is a word little used because it isn't understood or just isn't present. Florence Bulle has this to say in her very useful book:

"Because of Satan's uncanny ability to imitate, we need keen perception to differentiate between what is of God and what is not. Natural reasoning and logic are not enough. Spiritual discernment comes with spiritual maturity. To become mature we must go beyond the elementary teachings about Christ and constantly feed on the solid meat of the Word — the teaching about righteousness. In this way, the writer of Hebrews tells us, we train ouselves 'to distinguish good from evil'. We also need the spiritual discernment which comes as a *gift* of the Holy Spirit. God can and will supernaturally reveal evil which masks itself as good, so it is vitally important that we pray for this gift."*

* "God Wants You Rich — and Other Enticing Doctrines" by Florence Bulle (Bethany House Publishers, Minneapolis, Minnesota — 1983)

"I Never Knew You : Depart from me you Evildoers"

I believe those will be the chilling words heard by many who minister in churches today. Indeed having been in some where spiritualists have been ministering, I can say I would have little doubt. So often I have raised an eyebrow or made a comment and the reply has come back, as if it were some sort of criterion: "Well, were they ministering in *Jesus' name?*". These are the words of Jesus:

> *Not everyone that saith unto me, Lord, Lord, shall enter into the kingdom of heaven; but he that doeth the will of my Father which is in heaven.*
>
> *Many will say to me in that day, Lord, Lord, have we not prophesied* **in thy name?** *and in thy name have cast out devils? and in thy name done many wonderful works?*
>
> *And then will I profess unto them, I never knew you; depart from me, ye that work iniquity.*

(Matthew 7:21—23)

In her excellent little book on the subject of discernment with the telling title of "Let No Man Deceive You", Sue Waller addresses the questions. "Will I recognise a False Prophet? Living, as we do, before the ultimate exposure of that coming Day, are we confident that we will be able to recognise a false prophet? Will we in fact spot the wolf among the sheep? We may well wonder, in the face of the deceptive 'sheep's clothing', along with impressive miraculous works and subtle appealing teachings, if we will not be among those who are lured away from the truth and be deceived."*

Indeed let us not shy away from such questions. Let us fear God and search the Scriptures as we should, not supposing that everything is going to be easy. Sue Waller tells us that in order to discern whether a prophet is truly of God or not, we know that above all else we must look at the fruit being manifested in his life.

* "Let No Man Deceive You" by Sue Waller (New Wine Press, 1986)

As to his ministry, are there lasting results that bring glory to God? Alternatively has his ministry left confusion, division and a trail of tragedies in its wake?

It would be convenient for us to believe that we can know a false prophet by what he teaches, and no doubt we can if the error is that clear, but it is Jesus who tells us how to know a false prophet. He says: *"Ye shall know them by their fruits"* (Matthew 7:16).

Discernment of Error is not to Deny the Truth on which it is Based

This book is about the New Age error found in the true Church. It is about the seeds of wrong teaching fast growing in a rapidly expanding Church (the *true* Church) today. What this book is *not* seeking to do is to deny the truths on which some of the false teaching is based, nor is it the purpose to reject the relevance of the supernatural in the power of God.

We shall also look at *Inner Healing*. God certainly is the one who heals but we shall also be looking at Man's perversion of God's way. Again when we look at the *Prosperity Doctrine* it is no purpose to suggest that it is not God's will to meet all needs as He sees them. He promises to meet our *every* need. Our look at the *Shepherding movement* is not a denial of truly scriptural shepherding, and in examining all of these excesses the purpose is to allow God's truth to shine forth. To achieve that we have to expose the error that gets in its way and show the way of truth.

The book's purpose is to encourage the reader in his own discernment. At the outset let us be clear that the Bible is the *only* book of truth and inevitably there will be error somewhere in what I write. The Bible is a supernatural book, precise and perfect in every detail; my book is not. The Bible is the infallible Word of God, inerrant, complete and comprehensive. Every word, every jot and tittle is vital.

Warning those who do not love the truth, the Bible tells us: *"God shall send them a strong delusion, that they should believe a lie"* (2 Thessalonians 2:11). This book is to encourage Bible-believing Christians to recognise that delusion. There has always been delusion in the Church and the emphasis on "Bible-believing Christians" is made lest the view is taken that it is others, perhaps yesterday's people (and those professing Christians who remain in "dead" churches) who are referred to in the Scripture. In these days of ecumenism and "renewal" where we see compromise and respect for dead religion, I believe we need to look closely at what the delusion is *not*.

What the Delusion is Not!

It is for the reader to decide whether Paul was referring to the activities of organisations like the World Council of Churches when he writes of "a strong delusion".

Archbishop William Temple wrote a book called "Christianity and the Social Order" which was responsible in a large measure for swinging the churches of the post-war period towards Socialist and one-world thinking. In his book "The Fraudulent Gospel — Politics and the World Council of Churches", Bernard Smith tells us that it was Temple, then Archbishop of York, who presided over the Malvern Conference in 1942. It was attended by fifteen bishops and four hundred clergy and laymen, and one of its conclusions was:

"....The church can point to those features of our existing society which .... are contrary to divine justice, and act as stumbling blocks, making it harder for men to live Christian lives. In our present situation we believe that the maintenance of that part of the structure of our society by which the ultimate ownership of the principal industrial resources of the community can be vested in the hands of private owners may be such a stumbling block."*

Bernard Smith writes that Temple wanted the resolution

* "Foreign Affairs Publishing Co. Ltd — Richmond, Surrey (First Published 1977; Revised Edition 1979) Used by Permission.

to read that the vesting of principal industrial resources of the community in the hands of private owners *"is"* a stumbling block that makes it harder for men to live Christian lives. Enormously important as that was as a signal for the end times, this is not a book about politics, nor is it a book about the endless deceptions to be found in the *professing* church. Certainly there are true Christians in those places, and perhaps there were more of them in Archbishop Temple's day. Suffice to say William Temple became the Archbishop of Canterbury and the World Council of Churches of which he was the chief architect has moved from strength to strength in the spirit of the 1942 Malvern resolution. Some identify it as the main vehicle working by the spirit of Antichrist.

I have not made a study of William Temple, nor do I know the heart as God does. Some leaders among us today, who wrestle sincerely with the scriptures, qualify as Bible-believers, but have gone off on a tangent. William Temple, a man of a different day was maybe a leader of similar misfortune. We do not know. What we have today is men deceived in a different way. Like the men who teach, particularly on TV in the United States to multi-million audiences, that God wants us to be rich. Like Temple's message it is a popular one, but it is not the gospel which Jesus preached. We look at this idea that God wants us rich in the next chapter, "The Positive Confession Movement." Thus we commence Part Two where we examine five particular deceptions that are getting themselves firmly established in the Church.

Part Two

False Teaching in the Church

In *Part One* we have seen that the idea that we are "as gods" is the deception Satan continues to present to us. That is the deception. Passivity is the common cause of it.

In *Part Two* we examine five false teachings and are able to see how each one, in its own way, projects the same deception: "Ye are as gods".

In *Part Three* we shall see what are the vehicles being used and where, in the light of Scripture, the road can lead for those who do not have a *"love of the truth"* (2 Thessalonians 2:10). Is it to the idea of an earthly kingdom having much in common with what the New Age movement, the bride of Antichrist, is preparing?

In the false teaching we now examine are we seeing at least preparations for the "strong delusion" (2 Thessalonians 2:11) of which the Bible speaks?

We look at:

> Positive Confession
> Self-Esteem
> Inner Healing
> "Signs and Wonders"
> Holistic Health

What we see in each case is a distortion of a biblical truth. Before beginning *Part Two* it would be valuable to *ask the Lord* to reveal the deceptions, especially where there has been any personal involvement.

5

The Positive Confession Movement

The essence of teaching in the "Faith" movement seems to be that it is *always* God's will that we be healed and that we live in prosperity, or at any rate they say, "without lack" according to the standard of the society in which we are living. Failure to receive is often attributed by those in the movement to lack of faith, or perhaps a wrong confession. It is important positively to confess the healing, the prosperity or whatever the need. Hence the movement is called the "Positive Confession" movement. To acknowledge a cold or a headache is considered to be a *negative* confession and that is strongly discouraged. It is argued, from Scripture, that we are saved by confessing Christ as Saviour. Also true is that people in the Bible frequently confessed God and His power in accomplishing things. From there, they go on to say that just as we were saved we may also be healed by the same positive confession. The proof texts from Scripture brought to support this proposition were very convincing to me as I received Positive Confession teaching soon after my conversion as I desired to walk in faith. I soon came to understand the error as regards prosperity. It took longer as far as guaranteed healing was concerned.

Positive Attitudes are Desirable and Biblical

To have true faith is to trust God that He will do what He

has said He will do in His word.

All of Satan's deceptions are based upon a truth and there is of course *some* truth in the teaching of the Faith people because we are told to walk by faith. It is a basic requirement of the Christian walk. The Positive Confession idea is the first of the deceptions we look at and we shall need to establish from Scripture the basis for what may to some seem like an attack on the ministries of well-known men of God who "see results". However it is helpful first to establish some of the truths which are soundly based and are *not* being brought into question here. We *can* confess *positive* things and are encouraged to do so. But the emphasis is on *Christ*.

.... *The peace of God which passes all understanding shall guard my heart and my mind through* **Christ** *Jesus* (Philippians 4:7).

.... *I can do all things through* **Christ** *who strengthens me* (Philippians 4:13).

.... *I am crucified with* **Christ.** *I don't live but* **Christ** *lives in me* (Galatians 2:20).

These confessions are ones that accord with His will, but even so they have to be considered in the context of all the Word and not lifted out of context or "claimed" with the intellect. The revelation of the truth by the power of the Holy Spirit is absolutely necessary. Of course the Scripture texts on which the above confessions are based will seem to many, as they did to me, to be no different in type from the proof texts selected in the Positive Confession movement. It took me some good time before a *love* of the truth brought me to the place where I could see that the three examples above are better selections than, for example, 3 John 2, the text appearing on the cover of the current issue of the magazine sent out by my one-time "Faith" teacher as I write this chapter: *"Beloved. I wish above all things that thou mayest prosper and be in health, even as thy soul prospereth."* Interpreting that previously, I had been **selecting** scripture. I had followed what my teacher had called the "plain meaning" of the text. I had seized on that

76

and other proof texts, "claiming" them as God's will for me. But I **didn't** have the "plain meaning" of the text. As a new Christian I didn't know — and without good teaching a mature Christian might not know either — that the Greek word "prosper" in the Authorised Version means "to go well with someone" just as a friend might wish for things "to go well". I didn't take note that what I was reading was the second sentence in a letter to Gaius from his friend John, and so I missed what was really the "plain meaning".

What I had read was the standard form of greeting in a personal letter of that time. In the words of Dr. Gordon D. Fee, a Professor of the New Testament: "To extend John's wish for Gaius to refer to financial and material prosperity for all Christians of all times is *totally foreign* to the text. John neither intended that, nor could Gaius have so understood it. Thus it cannot be the 'Plain Meaning' of the text."*

Contending for the Faith (Jude 3) — Soundly Based in Scripture

False teachers had crept in to seduce and Jude warned that we *"earnestly contend for the faith which was once delivered unto the saints."* In another place Paul tells the elders at Ephesus about the attack expected on the Gospel coming from outside. He follows that with warning about men from the Christian ranks themselves.

For I know this, that after my departing shall grievous wolves enter in among you, not sparing the flock.

Also of your own selves shall men arise, speaking perverse things, to draw away disciples after them.

(Acts 20:29—30)

Paul warns against being tossed to and fro by every wind of doctrine. As a new Christian I was tossed to and fro by

---

* "The Disease of the Health and Wealth Gospels" by Gordon D. Fee ("The Word for Today" Publishers, Costa Mesa, CA, Reprinted: Agora Ministries, Costa Mesa — 1979)

"Faith" teaching.

> *That we henceforth be no more children, tossed to and fro and carried about with every wind of doctrine, by the sleight of men, and cunning craftiness, whereby they lie in wait to deceive.* (Ephesians 4:14)

There may be no intent to deceive, but the effect is to misrepresent Scripture. Having been deceived, what was I to do about it? Matthew 18:15—17 seemed somewhat difficult to apply to my "Faith" teacher, a man with an international ministry resident thousands of miles away in America, but anyway whether going to one's brother applied on a doctrinal matter I wasn't clear.

I did make early contact with the office of the "Faith" teacher, but I believe that when we are contending *for the faith itself* the procedure laid down by Scripture is found in Paul's treatment of Hymenaeus and Philetus in his Second Epistle to Timothy. Paul's words could properly apply to the Positive Confession teachers of our day. He wrote:

> *But shun profane and vain babblings: for they will increase unto more ungodliness.*
>
> *And their word will eat as doth a canker: of whom is Hymenaeus and Philetus;*
>
> *Who concerning the truth have erred, saying that the resurrection is past already; and overthrow the faith of some.* (2 Timothy 2:16—18)

Also Revelation 2:2 clearly expects us to test all those claiming any apostolic or travelling ministry. The test has to be Scripture.

Name-it-and-Claim-it!

As a young Christian I did not know my Bible at all well. I knew only bits and pieces of it. Even my head knowledge was minimal but what I lacked was the need also to understand the importance of the tenor of scripture, and unfortunately I concentrated much on teaching from the one who I have been describing as my favourite "Faith teacher".

After attending a conference featuring this man and his

wife I read "Faith" books and heard "Faith" tapes. It is true that *"faith cometh by hearing, and hearing by the word of God"* (Romans 10:17) but it is the Holy Spirit who has to give the interpretation. For my part I heard the message that "God's will is Prosperity". It seemed very relevant to my situation and needs. At the end of one conference session on this subject I put a very large amount in the very large bin that was passed around. The caution was that if I sowed sparingly I would reap sparingly (2 Corinthians 9:6). My £20 note was to be a seed. The Word spoke of seed sown on good soil to produce a crop thirty, sixty or even a hundred times what was sown (Mark 4:20). Modestly, I thought, I was believing God for *just* a *thirty*-fold return in accordance with the Word that had been sown in my heart! I was believing for the return that I thought was promised in the Word and the only barrier between me and my inheritance would be the lack of faith for £600. The idea was obviously attractive, and for those who can get their *minds* to work there can be results. However I didn't know the snags as I tried to receive the message in faith. I didn't know such ideas had no grounding in Scripture and what Satan was doing was seeking to re-introduce me to a subtle form of the *mind-power* I had known in the occult realm.

Later, on the same financial theme, I heard the testimony of the wife of this teacher. She saw that she had the "authority" over the house she wanted and over the money she needed to purchase it. All she had to do was take the authority "in the name of Jesus" over the money she needed (calling out the specific amount) and "command" it to come to her in Jesus' name. We have already met the lie that is at the root of this in chapter two. It is the lie that we are gods, that we have dominion and are able to subdue the earth and its resources. Not only does the teaching over-throw the biblical way of making a humble petition (called supplication) to God, replacing this with an idea of "God's laws", but it encourages mind power methods not taught in the Bible but used extensively in occult practices for getting needs met.

Some time after my introduction to this teaching and losing my £20 I reasoned that the teaching would be easily and understandably misinterpreted, that really I just didn't have the faith for the return on my gift and my attitude had been wrong. I came to the place of deciding that I hadn't grasped all of the teaching properly. In due course, prompted by a regular monthly mailing that majored on prosperity teaching, and aware also of my fairly dismal financial situation, I determined to make a careful and detailed study of *all* the scriptures this teacher had on various occasions given.

I completed this study and was very satisfied with the results. I set them out in a carefully typed form extending to many pages. It was nearly all Scripture with just short narratives linking the Bible verses together. It was as good a rationale as any I had seen, and very pleased I was!

Next, through what I later took to be God's provision, I received a telephone call from a friend who knew nothing of what I had been up to and nothing of my familiarity with this particular teacher's regular mailings. He had telephoned (and he didn't usually telephone) to tell me that the Lord had shown him this particular teacher was led by the spirit of Antichrist. Remember anti-Christ doesn't mean *against* Christ but *other* Christ. I listened carefully and we both agreed not to comment but to go away and pray about it. In a few days time I telephoned my friend. I hadn't yet found God's discernment on this and told him that I didn't witness with him. It was during that call that he gave me the scripture that I believed was remarkably to confirm that I should make a trip to the United States — the one described in the first chapter. As we have already seen, that visit didn't dispose of my involvement with the "Faith" message right away. However it was the key to it and in America I was handed the tape that boldly announced "You don't have a god in you; you *are* one."

It is in the nature of this kind of teaching that most often the error is subtly concealed. As the delusion grows such concealment is less necessary. I don't say that the absence of such a bold statement on the same teacher's thousands of tapes in the United Kingdom is necessarily deliberate; we wrestle not against flesh and blood but with the deceptions of the spiritual realm. The teaching comes from the United States. We can expect the spirit of delusion might be stronger there. The need for embroidering this particular message is surely less in a country where there is round-the-clock Christian TV that focuses heavily on the ''Faith'' message reaching multi-millions at peak-viewing times.

The 30- 60- 100- and the 1000-Fold Return!

No sooner had I written these words about the way a message tends to be more boldly stated when ministered in the United States, than I had occasion to attend a large crusade on a showground very near to my home. The preacher was from the third world and he had appeared at many conferences becoming very well known in the early part of the year; a reputation had gone ahead of him because he had been used to raise numerous people from the dead.

On this occasion I was to be present at the most extra-ordinary demonstration of outrageous tomfoolery and soulish ministry that I had ever anywhere witnessed at a Christian gathering. Yet, excepting the discerning few, hundreds were spell-bound. For my part, after the main text of this book had been finished, I was seeing for the first time in a single ministry so much of what is written in these pages. I give a single example from this ministry.

I choose the example of the 1000-fold return. When follow-ing the Positive Confession teaching myself I was made very familiar with the scriptures which were interpreted to promise a return of 30-, 60- and 100-fold on our giving. I had never ''gone for the 100''! Rather I rationalised that I didn't yet have the faith for that. I praise God that as I took these scriptures out of their context my financial situation actually got worse! Now here was a man with a 1000-fold return! What next?

First our distinguished visitor called for what was quite a large and specified number of people (and he got many more than the number) who would make what on any view was a very large gift. Then, with the list complete it was time for the prayer and the command to the Heavenly Father:

"Father I ask for surprising miracles for these ones. We command these return a thousand fold."

Returning home from the showground, I was able to read the magazine I had been given by the Ministry, and I was reminded of a quotation from one recent book from America. It read: "Until we comprehend that we are little gods and we begin to act like little gods, we cannot manifest the Kingdom of God." I read in the magazines that the influential American who penned those words was to be the principal invited speaker at the special celebration to be held at the opening of the new church complex of the man I had been listening to.

The teaching common today, including that of this American who covers various ministries and churches, is "…. that the church must take over the world and establish the Kingdom of God upon earth; and only then Christ will return, not to catch us up to meet him IN THE AIR and to take His bride to Heaven; but He will return TO EARTH to reign over the Kingdom we have established for Him. This is the old Manifested Sons doctrine that was declared a heresy by the Assemblies of God in 1950."*

The speaker had left the showground mid-evening bound for America. I was again reminded that the earth is these days a small place, that powerful ideas and words knew no boundaries and that it seemed quite inevitable that teaching that "works" in America can quickly take a hold in Britain. I could see too that what the New Agers call "networking" (the simple thing these days of "keeping in touch") operated on the Christian scene too.

* Letter — Dave Hunt (November 1985)

"We are Little Gods"

What we have in the scene described above is a misunder-
standing of what is the Kingdom of God. This is coupled
with the doctrine of the manifestation of the sons of God.
We are not ''little gods'' and we are not to ''act like little
gods'', and we have looked at the serpent's proposition that
''ye are as gods'' in chapter two. Neither are we to feed off
the soulish, psychic power — the passive mind which neglects
the word of God — which was evident in the above example
and which we have seen in chapter three. This way we can
avoid false notions and any wrong expectations that we shall
''manifest the Kingdom of God''. We find the same wrong
ideas entering passive minds time and again, and in this book
we are examining the errors and teaching that result. In
chapter eleven we shall look at Shepherding/Discipleship,
a vehicle that has been used for the doctrines. In chapters
twelve, thirteen and fourteen, looking more closely at the
manifestation of the sons of God and the ''Kingdom'', the
consequences of the ''passive mind'' and the teaching that
''ye are as gods'' can be seen.

The truth is we are awaiting expectantly for the return of
our Lord in the air (1 Thessalonians 4:17). It is *then* that
the sons of God will be manifest (Romans 8:19). These
biblical doctrines are neglected by growing numbers of
Christian leaders. They don't want to contend for the faith
(Jude 3) if that means dividing over doctrine. Rather many
are poised to unite, to take over the world, and to establish
God's Kingdom here and now. We may ask the question:
Are the New Age people and these ''Kingdom'' people
headed to the same goal? Let us be encouraged in our discernment through spending time with the Word; Paul writes to
the Thessalonians not only about Christ's return but also
about Antichrist who must be revealed in the flesh. Will these
false teachers come to realise that it is Antichrist's kingdom
they are in all innocence helping to establish? Will they
recognise Antichrist when he is revealed in the flesh?

The 90-Foot Jesus

Will we recognise the false Christ when he appears?

The Lord has used many ministries to bring souls to Him. Oral Roberts has been described as the grandfather of television evangelists. The story of a vision he describes is well-known. He had a vision of Jesus ninety feet high. He shared with his television audience and the money poured in to build his City of Faith hospital complex. The hospital was built and is operational.

There will be those like myself who find no scriptural warrant for many of the testimonies of visions of Jesus that we hear. I have been in meetings myself where the sight of Jesus has been claimed, but I saw no-one fall on his face before Him. However, often we can only wait upon the Lord and see what further He has to show us.

What does seem clear is that the Prosperity Gospel looked at previously involves a treadmill of financial servicing that requires ever more funds as the scale of operation increases. Television is the way to those funds. As with any business, there are on-going expenses to be met or soon in the words of one religious news reporter there is a "90-foot bill collector standing at the door and knocking loudly."*

I can only faithfully report Oral Roberts' own appeals, and I do that so we may weigh up doctrine against Scripture. He has told television viewers of his further financial needs. This time, I believe, the doctrinal error, apart from the financial aspect, relates not to a 90-foot Jesus but to the subject of physical death. The New York Religious News Service (RNS) reported (7th January 1987):

"For the second time since last March, evangelist Oral Roberts has warned that he may die if he can't raise $8 million to provide full scholarships for students at his medical school in Tulsa, Oklahoma."

The evangelist, a United Methodist, told television viewers Jan 4 that he has already raised $3.5 million. But he added

* Clark Morphew on Religion (St. Paul Pioneer and Press — 10 January 1987)

84

that if the full $8 million is not raised by March of this year, 'God could call Oral Roberts home'."

Does God have such a price? Jesus has paid the price. We are redeemed by His blood. Once again I find no scriptural warrant for this brother to be called home on such a basis. We each must have discernment for ourselves but this doesn't sound like the Jesus of the Bible.

What Another "Faith" Teacher has to say

Faith is important to each one of us. We all need it. It comes from a proper understanding of the Word of God through having a correct interpretation of it written on our hearts by the Holy Spirit.

Jimmy Swaggart is a Faith teacher and in his book "Hyper-Faith: a New Gnosticism?" he has described some "Faith" ministries as a new gnosticism. The teachers of gnosticism in the time of the early Church took what they considered the most attractive teachings of ancient Greece, Judaism and the Eastern cultures, and incorporated them into Christianity. They were tapping into the tree of knowledge. Swaggart writes that it is very difficult to gain a grasp of the philosophy from which the corrupted teaching comes without understanding this description of gnosticism. He refers to the philosophy of E.W. Kenyon, already referred to in chapter two and from which "Faith" teaching comes. Along with men like William Branham whose ministry is looked at in some detail in chapter twelve the Kenyon teaching has its roots in the Manifest Sons of God doctrine. Jimmy Swaggart summarises the "Faith" position very clearly where he writes:

"Their basic difficulty with the Word of God is that they separate the Word from the person of the Lord Jesus Christ. In short they have replaced God with their chosen scriptures, rationalising that this will justify their actions. The words of scripture are deified — apart from the living God — and exalted into various "laws", which bring the forces of good and evil into action."*

The Truth or the Positive?

When we leave the truth to concentrate on "positive" goals sorcery is not far away. The title of the next section is "Sorcery" and in the above quotation from Jimmy Swaggart there is found the clear clue, the idea that there is power in words. E.W. Kenyon taught that Jesus was always positive in His message but while Jesus looks on our hearts, at the heart of the Positive Confession message is getting the words right and keeping *them* positive.

In "Beyond Seduction"** Dave Hunt writes, "what actually matters is not whether something is 'positive' but whether something is true or false, biblical or not biblical. In that context, then, the terms 'positive' or 'negative" are not only irrelevant but a smokescreen that obscures real issues." Referring to the *"strong delusion"* to believe Satan's lie (2 Thessalonians 2:9—12) about which Paul warned those who were not lovers of the truth, Hunt continues: "The popular substitution of 'positive' for 'truth' is a perfect set-up for the prophesied delusion."

Isn't it perfectly clear that the Bible, positive for the gospel it contains, is cram full of negatives which men ignore at their peril? Isn't it certain that Genesis 2:17 contains a vital *negative*? It reads:

> But the tree of the knowledge of good and evil, thou shalt not eat of it: for in the day that thou eatest thereof thou shalt surely die.

For a *positive* biblical verse we can read on to Genesis 3:5. What could be more positive than the serpent's promise to Eve that she would become a god through eating the forbidden fruit, a promise accepted by the cults and actually coming from Satan?

---

* "Hyper-Faith: A New Gnosticism?" by Jimmy Swaggart (Jimmy Swaggart Ministries, Baton Rouge, LA — 1982)
** Published by Harvest House, Eugene, Oregon — 1987

More and more Christians believe this lie. The scripture is presented throughout this book with a proper interpretation. It is a positive scripture and many are seizing it and treating is as such. Yet they mistake the truth. *All* scripture is the truth. Scripture contains positives and negatives. It is not true that we ''shall be as gods'', and it is out of that *positive* statement that result all the so-called *positive* things identified in this book. Positive methods, techniques and therapies have flowed from Man's search for the positive in scripture, but that is not the biblical way. *''**All** scripture is given by inspiration of God and is profitable for .... reproof, for correction ....''* (2 Timothy 3:16).

If scripture is to be used for reproof and correction, isn't it clear that much warning and many negatives will be found? It is in the cause of contending for the faith and encouraging a seeking after the truth that much in these pages is negative rather than positive, yet we may express the meaning of positive in another way. We have said the Bible is positive in the sense that it is the Gospel; as a *whole* it is the *whole* truth. As we identify and cast out error, we are bringing souls nearer to the *whole* truth.

Sorcery

There is a clear line to be drawn between Holy Spirit ministries and sorcery. The experience from America shows that not only are Christian ministries very close to or over that line but also that they are hardly distinguishable from those which have never been on the Christian side. Napoleon Hill is one who has a following among Christians and, as Hunt and McMahon point out,* it is interesting that Christians recommending his writings (His famous title is ''Think and Grow Rich''), if offering any caution, do so as regards the *wealth* aspect. The dangers of the mind power involved pass undiscerned. Peace of mind can be dangerous when it is counterfeit; my own embarkation into the occult

* see ''The Seduction of Christianity''

began with counterfeit peace of mind. In his book, "Grow Rich with Peace of Mind" Napoleon Hill describes the "unseen friends" that sometimes "hover" about him. He has discovered there is a group of strange beings who maintain a school of wisdom with "Masters" who can disembody themselves and travel instantly to wherever they choose. Sadly Napoleon Hill is tapped into the occult realm.

Hill's "Positive Mental Attitudes" are close to those of another group, the "Positive Possibility Thinkers". Dave Hunt tells us that these have their roots in "New Thought", a group which emphasised that thought controlled everything. "The power of thinking, whether negative or positive, was believed to be sufficient even to create physical reality or to destroy it. God was not personal, but a Great Mind which was activated by our thoughts and would actualise them into concrete form. The corollary of this axiom is obvious: Man is divine."* He tells us this was once forced out of the church as a heresy only to survive in cults like Christian Science. "Today's church is being swept by a revival of New Thought, now called Positive Thinking, Positive Confession, Positive Mental Attitude, and Inner Healing. We are very concerned that this time New Thought, which represents inside the church what New Age is in the secular world, will not be forced out, but will remain within the Evangelical Church to contribute to the growing confusion and seduction. One of the most basic New Thought techniques is visualisation, which is now firmly entrenched within the church."*

Error: Difficult to see when involved

Of all the errors invading the church today and described in this book, the Positive Confession ("Faith") teaching was the last I was to discern. That is because I was so involved with it as a Christian. As with all these things, it is not easy to see the error when once we are involved, excepting God's grace and our determination to seek after the truth. We are

* "The Seduction of Christianity"

to confess our sin, but there is no place in the Christian life for the Word power and confession of our needs as taught in the Positive Confession Movement. Positive Confession is an invitation, sooner or later, to get some answers, but they will not necessarily be *God's* answers to prayer. God meets our needs in His way in accordance with His Word because we keep His commandments and do what is pleasing in His sight. It is necessary that we are convicted of our sin. We can repent and move on in our walk with God. It is a mark of the Positive Confession Movement, and of the other teachings that avoid mention of sin in the self-centred gospels of today, that conviction is really seen as condemnation. How often we hear, "There is no condemnation for those who are in Christ Jesus". Sin remains under cover. The emphasis is on experience rather than on *repentance*. The answers are sought through experiences rather than through *repentance*. It is as Jimmy Swaggart has written of the Positive Confession people, "If you will notice, their leaders seldom preach against any kind of sin."* These leaders would do well to remember that we still have the flaws and inconsistencies of humans, and only God's grace and mercy — through Jesus Christ — allow us to enter the presence of God. We are not like the gnostics who taught that we couldn't have a human nature *and* a godly nature at the same time. The truth is that we can and we do. We *are* human. We seek to keep filled with the Holy Spirit. But we *do* sin. Through Jesus we can *confess* our *sin* and be forgiven.

Let us contend for the faith. Let us trust that our brothers and sisters in the Lord know they are as fallible as we are ourselves. Let us trust they love the truth as much as we do. Let us trust they will want to have error, or possible error, pointed out through a signalling of Bible truth to them. Whilst we don't favour unity at the expense of the truth, let us trust that others don't either, and let us trust God to quicken the truth to others where we point to it.

* "Hyper-Faith: A New Gnosticism?"

Jimmy Swaggart, whom I have quoted above in the context of his good discernment of the Positive Confession movement, is much used of the Lord particularly in America where he has sold millions of Christian records. Yet we are *all* vulnerable. The great need for each one of us is that we realise we *can* be deceived. Hardly believing a copy of a vision I received and which bore Swaggart's name, I wrote to him and the tape* I received in reply was a clear confirmation. It seems God told Jimmy that He had appointed *his* ministry as He had appointed *"no other ministry"*, to help gather the harvest! "You must do it by television", he was told. "This is the only way that millions can be reached in a short period of time …. this ministry is the only one I have anointed to reach the whole world — and television is the only way to get it done." Yes his ministry is anointed, but surely not to the exclusion of all others?

In chapter seven we shall meet another American TV evangelist. He has met with Jesus who told him He wanted his TV network to get the first shots of His return to earth!

Yet we can all be deceived, we can deceive others and we can cause much confusion. For my own part the excesses of the Positive Confession teaching I received had their consequences too.

My Positive Confession!

I described my own confusion in a News Letter I published and which read as follows:

"My book, 'Understanding Alternative Medicine — Health Care in the New Age', published in 1985, included *Parts One to Four* which amounted to almost a blanket warning against alternative medicine as we know it today. At that time I did not understand that what I had written in those *four parts* was really positive in that it directed readers away from Satan's counterfeits. Further I didn't understand that the much bandied words, 'positive' and 'negative', don't appear

* tape — "The Fields are White for Harvest" (Jimmy Swaggart)

in Scripture and that what is significant is "truth". We are to be "lovers of the truth" (2 Thessalonians 2:10). Could it be that the cry for positive things that is everywhere heard, is really a mistaken one? Could the focus on the positive even be led from below to get our attention away from the truth? Don't we see that Christians are being so "positive" today they are even receiving the positive statement from the serpent (Genesis 3:5)? Isn't that lie of the serpent the one at the heart of what the "positive confession" people are teaching? The Bible says something which is very "negative": *"for in the day that thou eatest thereof thou shalt surely die"* (Genesis 2:17). The importance lies in the fact that it is God's word and that it is true.

Whatever the answers, my purpose here is to refer to *Part Five* of "Understanding Alternative Medicine". In this final section I dealt with the subject of "Divine Healing". After four so-called negative sections, I thought I had better be positive, providing the true alternative for the holistic therapies I was dismissing. I fell into the trap the enemy had set as I spent dozens of hours at "Positive Confession" meetings, listening to tapes and reading the glossy books filled with scriptures plucked out of their proper context. That reflects in Part Five of my book. I apologise to my readers and ask them to forgive me. Maybe some will see no fault. Indeed for my own part I still have to seek the Lord for a clearer revelation from His word so that I may discern the extent to which the positive confession excesses have penetrated my writing and my understanding. I do urge you to please pray, and to those who will rejoice that I am at last seeing the light in this area, I should value prayers both for a greater understanding and in regard to the books in circulation and still being sold."

We need to keep the truth of human nature in mind. The standard is to be found in only one place — the Bible. It is the inerrant Word of God. Human nature will ever be with us until Jesus returns **in the air.** Jesus, having told us not to worry about what we shall eat, drink or wear, and reminding us that it is the pagans who run after these things, tells us: *"But seek ye first the Kingdom of God, and his righteousness; and all these things shall be added unto you"* (Matthew 6:33). With His own first coming, the Kingdom has been inaugurated. With His second coming it will be fully consummated. Let us reject the idea that the confession of the believer (acting as a god) can control the world around him. The Manifest Sons of God believe that very thing and that Christ's return is a return *in them*. As gods *they* will establish the Kingdom ready for one who will, after all, not be Jesus Christ but Antichrist in the flesh. Let us keep in mind that Positive Confession, "Faith" and Word teaching is rooted in that message, rather than in literal fundamentalism as supposed.

In "Beyond Seduction" published in 1987 a brief reference to Manifest Sons of God teaching is made. The book deals very thoroughly with Positive Confession and Self Esteem teaching in a way that can't be covered with a book such as this. The Manifest Sons message, we are told, is a logical extension of Positive Confession teaching. Then looking at the broader Christian scene, Dave Hunt reported two significant observations by a Manifest Sons publication in America:

1. The belief in the Rapture among mainline denominations was waning.
2. Increasing numbers of Christians were discovering, what the publication called, the Bible's New Age principles of ruling and reigning here on earth.

I know that the names of Kenyon and the Manifest Sons of God will be new to many who will read this book. Positive Confession doctrine originated with Kenyon and like other errors highlighted the destination that is signalled is in the doctrine of the Manifest Sons of God. These and various other names are introduced in various chapters. I could have dealt with each of these separately but presenting them in this way, I believe the interdependence of so much of the error can be better seen. A clearer picture of how farreaching the error is and how much New Age teaching has come into the Church will be presented. Notwithstanding that, the Manifestation of the Sons of God, a far-reaching subject about which very little has been written, is looked at in some detail in chapter twelve. In the next chapter we consider ''Self-esteem'', another false teaching which leads in the same direction.

6

Another Gospel : Self Esteem and Psychology

In the previous chapter we have looked at Positive Confession and described it as "error". Cult expert, Professor Walter Martin, describes* the self-esteem taught by Robert Schuller as The *Cult* of Self Esteem. Schuller says he sees himself as a sort of "Carnival Barker" getting the crowds into his church where they later receive the "Gospel". His forum is a TV programme called the "Hour of Power" watched by three or four million viewers each week. In the previous chapter we have seen two different meanings for the expression "plain meaning". Whenever we look at doctrine the meaning of words is of critical importance. Just as we find in the Roman Catholic church, those like Martin who have studied Schuller's teaching very carefully have found an entirely new gospel covered over by the use of familiar words. However first let us once again take the step of examining the truth that has been perverted and so avoid going out of balance as we identify the error.

It is not wrong to promote self-esteem in the context of being a child of God. We should love our neighbour *as we love ourselves* (Leviticus 19:18).

It is not wrong for Christians to think positively in relation to themselves and God. *We can do all things through Christ who strengthens us* (Philippians 4:13). Like the Positive Confession of the "Faith" teachers, "Possibility Thinking" is the tool of the Gospel of Self Esteem, but

* Walter Martin's tape: "Robert Schuller and the Cult of Self Esteem" (C.R.I. — San Juan Capistrano, CA)

instead the positive thought has to be "Thy Will be Done" and the sovereignty of God, and His grace, not the 'possibilities' of our faith.

It is not wrong in the life of the Christian to strive for possibilities of faith if it means trusting God. We should be trusting God and there are scriptures where the Lord does encourage these possibilities. We can be sure the Bible is a *balanced revelation* presenting a consistent message against which the Gospel of Self-Esteem can be measured.

It is in the definitions of sin, hell, pride, the new birth, etc that the problem is most easily understood. However it is impossible to do justice to extraordinary definitions provided by Dr. Schuller in a short chapter. Self-esteem, seen as a virtue, is reckoned to be the single greatest need facing the human race today. Hence the Gospel of Self Esteem. Here are some definitions:

"Self-esteem then, or 'pride in being a human being', is the single greatest need facing the human race today ....

Do not fear pride: the easiest job God has is to humble us. God's almost impossible task is to keep us believing every hour of every day how great we are as his sons and daughters on planet earth."*

In the words of Professor Walter Martin, President of the renowned Christian Research Institute concluding his excellent cassette tape:

"People hear it, mistake the vocabulary and think that it's Christianity when it's a complete counterfeit of the Gospel"**

In distinction to Schuller's position the Bible has this to say:
> *Yea, all of you be subject one to another, and be clothed with humility: for God resisteth the proud, and giveth grace to the humble.* (1 Peter 5:5)
> *But he giveth more grace, Wherefore he saith, God*

---

* 'Self-Esteem: The New Reformation'' by Dr Robert Schuller (Waco, TX: Word Books 1982)
** "Robert Schuller and the Cult of Self-Esteem" (tape) by Walter Martin (C.R.I. — San Juan Capristrano, CA)

resisteth the proud, but giveth grace unto the humble.
                                                    (James 4:6)
   Pride goeth before destruction, and an haughty spirit
before a fall.   (Proverbs 16:18)

Christianity today is invaded by the ideas of what Man wants and how it is normal for Man to behave. The Bible is being challenged unknowingly by the most well-meaning of Christians, conditioned by their experiences and by the circumstances of their daily lives. Social life is fast-changing. Life in the home is changing. Life in the workplace is greatly changed. The Bible way is being challenged head on and from every direction by Man's way. At most theological colleges and seminaries psychology is a recognised subject. This has not long been so, but today the truth of God's Word is not considered to be enough to govern the behaviour of many sincere Christians. We now have psychology, the study of "how man behaves when he doesn't have God." I have never found a better simple definition than that. Psychology — how unredeemed *natural* Man behaves — has become blurred by the *supernatural.* Both pave the way for a Man-centred gospel with lying signs and wonders.

Self Esteem: The New Reformation!

The year 1982 saw the publication of the important new book in the United States already referred to. It was "Self Esteem: The New Reformation" by Dr. Robert Schuller. The main thesis of this, seen too in earlier books by the same author, is that our problem, and every ill that plagues society, is the result of having a low self-esteem. Therefore, the argument runs, the greatest need is that self-esteem be increased.

   Before we look further at Dr. Schuller's ministry let us be clear that even critics who are engaged in exposing error through national ministries in America will acknowledge that Schuller is a *Christian* minister who *does* believe in the Gospel of Jesus Christ. However the *fact* seems to be, in the words of Joseph P. Gudel: "The prime focus of Dr. Schuller's ministry today concerns the self-esteem of the individual. This was reflected in most of his earlier books, but was never specifically formulated until 1982, when he wrote 'Self-Esteem: The New Reformation' ''*

For my own part I needed to look no further than the foreword of one of the books put into my hand as soon as I had been saved. I didn't consider the foreword carefully then. It was written by a man little known in Britain, Robert Schuller! One day the foreword got my attention! I read that the writer had discovered the reality of that dynamic dimension in prayer that comes through *visualising* the healing experience. ''Time'' magazine tells us that this American is watched on nearly two hundred TV stations each Sunday by an audience of nearly three million. His TV programme has become the most widely watched televised church service in America, he receives between thirty thousand and forty thousand letters a week, and has a mailing list of over one million people. He has written very many books and several have been best-sellers. More than 20,000 church leaders have attended his courses on successful church leadership. Such is the potential to mislead by a man with immense influence.

In Schuller's early ministry he saw the church as a place where non-Christians would be attracted and where they would later accept Jesus. His ideas came from the ''Positive Thinking'' school which had come on to the Christian scene, and the foundations for his own style of ''Possibility Thinking'' were laid. Positive thinking in turn came from the Positive Mental Attitude movement in the secular world. We need to trace roots and sometimes they run deep. However these methods are described, the root of the idea is that Man can control the course of his life by mental processes and that, by his thoughts, he can bring into his experience whatever he desires. The gospel is one of success, signs and wonders, and self-esteem.

---

* From ''A New Reformation?'' by Joseph P. Gudel (''Forward'' Magazine, CRI California-Spring 1985)

Low Self-Esteem and Inferiority are Quite Different

Self-esteem teaching, by its very name evidencing a mighty threat to the best of Christian values, is making great headway. In the spiritual realm where the battle is, this false doctrine is helped along by confusion. The confusion results from the failure to see the difference between how we view our *abilities* (which can be improved) and how we view our *self-esteem* (which we should *not* seek to improve).

We may not be good performers; some may have a very low level of ability and there is an area here for improvement. Inferiority feelings can creep in or even be deep seated, and there is no scriptural justification for these. However there *are* steps that can be taken so that we can become better performers to the glory of God. Self-esteem is not the opposite of inferiority. It is not to be the aim to increase *self*-worth when we are less able or less capable of performing various skills; the aim is to show increase in the ways we serve *God* and our *fellow men*. *Self*-esteem relates to self-worth, and the constant battle of the Christian life is to die to self. It is hard to grasp. I find it difficult to live out. Yet we can know it is God's perfect way for us. I am not to feel inferior and I am to improve my performance where I am able. Neither am I to esteem myself let alone seek to increase my self-esteem. It is as we die to self that God can use us more.

Except we understand the importance in God's plan of dying to self the difference between inferiority and lack of self-esteem can never be discerned. Surely the Gospel of Self-Esteem preached more and more openly in these days both reflects the confusion of this difference and the failure of its teachers to understand God's plan for their lives.

Visualisation

We now take a look at another area of deception where

confusion abounds. Just as abilities can be increased whilst self-esteem should be discouraged, visions can be from God but the increasing ways of visualisation have to be discouraged also.

God gives *visions* as He wills. *Visualisation* is when *we* get our visions for *ourselves* or with the help of others. Having grabbed at all the positives the world has to offer, believing them all to come from God, how much more readily will men delight in the supernatural experiences they are given? Christians must understand the techniques which belong to New Thought and Positive Thinking. If we accept that the New Age is the preparation for the powerful delusion of which the Bible speaks (2 Thessalonians 2:11) then we can expect the New Thought techniques may well remain part of the scene in the Church.

Dave Hunt, in common with all others who are experienced in the ways of the occult, emphasises time and again in "The Seduction of Christianity" the enormous significance of visualisation. He quotes New York Academy of Science anthropologist, Michael Harner who puts visualisation at the top of the list of psychospiritual technologies that represent a revival of shamanism. Shamanism is sorcery or witchcraft. Harner defines a shaman as a man or woman who enters an altered state of consciousness — at will — to contact and utilise an ordinarily hidden reality in order to acquire knowledge, power, to help others, etc. In "The Way of the Shaman" Harner joins hands with a distinguished Australian anthropologist to drive home his point that the vision of the aborigine shaman is not an hallucination but "a mental formation visualised and externalised, which may exist for a time independent of its creator." Of course what is seen is a manifestation of demons. They have been invited in, through the mind, by visualisation, and the easiest way to get lies established in Man's mind is to visualise them. Things are always more readily understood with the help of pictures. But, the reader may ask, why should a visualisation of something good be encouraged by demons?

Whilst visualisation is known and practised by pagan tribes, false religions, cults and people in the occult, the practice finds no warrant in Scripture. Our walk with the Lord is a walk in faith not one where we visualise Him.

For we walk by faith, not by sight (2 Corinthians 5:7). What we can visualise is not reality. If we are picturing a sick person recovered that is an act of the mind calling forth mind power. Nor can we even have a basis for any picture of Jesus we seek to conjure for we cannot know what Jesus looks like. Our joy as believers is to know His abiding presence.

God can of course give us visions, but they are as *He* wills, and there need be little difficulty in discerning the origins of pictures that are called forth intentionally out of Man's own mind. He has entered into passivity. In Genesis 6:5 we read that every imagination of the thoughts of Man's heart was only *"evil continually"*; the answer is not in imagination and visualisation.

Visualisation is psychical (Oxford Dic: "of the soul or mind"). Like the manifestation to the psychic, what we have is a powerful application of the mind. It is the way of the shaman and it is one of the most significant ways in which Satan, masquerading as an angel of light, is infiltrating the Church today.

The Man-Centred Gospel

David Wilkerson, pastor and author of "The Cross and the Switchblade", writing of the need for Christians to "flee from the land of the north" (Zechariah 2:6), identifies the close connection between secular positive thinking and the variation with the Christian label. He put it this way:

"What is this evil wind from the north the angel of God warns us to flee from? It is more than communism. It is more than secular humanism. Those are not the evils that have infiltrated God's house. God's greatest concern is the man-centred gospel now propagated by ministers and evangelists who are under the influence of this "wind from the north.""

There is an evil wind from the north blowing into God's house, deceiving multitudes of God's chosen people. It is a kind of humanism wrapped in scriptures. It is a scriptural take-off on Napoleon Hill's book *Think and Grow Rich*.

This perverted gospel seeks to make gods of people. They are told. 'Your destiny is in the power of your mind. Whatever you can conceive is yours. Speak it into being. Create it by a positive mind set. Success, happiness, perfect health is all yours — if you will only use your mind creatively. Turn your dreams into reality by using mind power.'

Let it be known once and for all. God will not abdicate His lordship to the power of our minds, negative or positive. We are to seek only the mind of Christ, and His mind is not materialistic: it is not focused on success or wealth. Christ's mind is focused only on the glory of God and obedience to His Word.

No other teaching so ignores the Cross and the corruption of the human mind. It bypasses the evil of our ruined Adam nature, and it takes the Christian's eye off Christ's gospel of eternal redemption and focuses it on earthly gain. Saints of God, flee from this wind from the north! It will lead you to despair and emptiness.''*

Psychology

While psychologists are passing on from their Man-centred studies into spiritual transpersonal psychology, Christians are getting sucked into the psychology system at the other end of the pipe line. These Christians, many of them already experiencing supernatural power in their ministries, must beware of the traps that can await even those who venture a single step into this most subtle deception. The way Man behaves if he doesn't walk with God is very different from the way when he does! Psychology and Christianity have little in common. They both seek to explain Man's behaviour but each has its own solution, and our caution against the methods of psychology is not any denial of the essential human element in Man.

* ''A Prophecy-Wall of Fire'' by David Wilkerson (October 1984)

Visiting America after renouncing Moral Re-Armarment (MRA) as a cult I asked Robert Vlerick, a teacher of Spiritual Warfare, the one who first identified the New Age Movement to me, if he knew any cult that was more subtle than MRA. His answer was immediate and without qualification: psychology. If the Bible is true then psychology only offers what we do not need. Psychology pretends to scientifically understand the heart of man, and so denies our spiritual nature and our free will. Psychology encourages us to improve ourselves rather than to submit ourselves broken and fit to be used by the living God. One doesn't have to be a Christian to know that pride abounds throughout the human race, but today according to much of the teaching the problem is supposed to lie in our **lack of self worth** or our **humility.**

We Don't Need to Learn to Love Ourselves

It is one problem when we fail to realise that God loves us, but it is quite another to suppose that we have to *learn* to love ourselves! Even people who appear to put themselves down are most often letting people know they haven't reached the standard they have set themselves. The truth is we *don't* hate ourselves. The Bible is quite clear on this.

For no man ever yet hated his own flesh; but nourisheth and cherisheth it, even as the Lord the church.

(Ephesians 5:29)

This verse states quite plainly that *no-one ever hated himself.* The implication is that those who think or say they hate themselves are actually covering up hidden pride.

To die to self must be the goal of all who follow Jesus in order that He might live in us. Psychology is the enemy of that purpose, and A.W. Tozer can be quoted to explain in a very clear way both the nature of self and how it is that self-derogation is a focus on self, "one of the toughest plants growing in the garden of life."

103

"Self-derogation is bad for the reason that self must be there to derogate. Self, whether swaggering or grovelling, can never be anything but hateful to God.

Boasting is an evidence that we are pleased with self; belittling, that we are disappointed in it. Either way we reveal that we have a high opinion of ourselves ....

The victorious Christian neither exalts nor down-grades himself. His interests have shifted from self to Christ. What he is or is not no longer concerns him. He believes he has been crucified with Christ and he is not willing either to praise or deprecate such a man ....

It (self) is in fact indestructible by any human means. Just when we are sure it is dead it turns up somewhere as robust as ever to trouble our peace and poison the fruit of our lives."*

Satan uses every means at his disposal to get us to eat from the tree of *knowledge* of good and evil. The tree of *life* is at our disposal. Jesus came that we might receive that life *in Him*. That life in Jesus is better than man's efforts; we want Jesus to fill our very lives. We can fill our minds with the Word, how we live with God; not with psychology, how we behave without Him.

Pride: A Deadly Sin

Even non-Christians recognise pride as a deadly sin and that all of human nature thinks too highly of itself. Yet now we have pastors telling us that the problem is not pride but humility!

What is low self-esteem but the flip side of pride? The answer to self-esteem, whether it be low or high, is to be rid of it and not build it up. Of course most of us do it, but once again it isn't the Christian way.

Concluding his excellent summary of the self-idolatry involved in self-esteem, Dave Hunt, in "The Seduction of Christianity" quotes William Law on the view held by the Church for centuries:

* "Man: the Dwelling Place of God" by A.W. Tozer (1897—1963) (STL Books, Bromley — 1981)

"Men are dead to God because they are living to Self. Self-love, self-esteem and self-seeking are the essence and the life of pride; and the Devil, the father of pride, is never absent from these passions, nor without an influence in them. Without a death to self there is no escape from Satan's power over us …. Imagination, as the last and truest support of self, lays unseen worlds at his feet, and crowns him with secret revenges and fancied honours. This is that satanic, natural self that must be denied and crucified, or there can be no disciple of Christ. There is no plainer interpretation than this that can be put upon the words of Jesus, *'Except a man deny self, and take up the cross and follow me, he cannot be my disciple.'* "*

And quoting Jesus' words from Luke's Gospel:

"If any man come to me and hate not …. his own life …. he cannot be my disciple. And whosoever doth not bear his cross and come after me, cannot be my disciple …. So likewise, whosoever he be of you that forsaketh not all that he hath, he cannot be my disciple".

Luke 14:26,27,33).

We are to deny self, reject the gospel of self-idolatry and self-esteem and follow Jesus.

* "The Power of the Spirit" by William Law (Christian Literature Crusade, 1971) Ed. Dave Hunt.

7
Inner Healing

In the charismatic environment of my early life as a Christian I had a very uneasy feeling about Inner Healing, though for a long time I was unable to articulate to others just precisely what my reservations about this ministry were. I had seen various people ministered to and had heard what seemed exciting testimonies from those apparently blessed by "Inner Healing". This often included "going back to the womb" and "visualisation". In one testimony the subject was wrapped tightly with a blanket over her face in order to simulate the womb situation; in another the heating was turned up higher.

In one case I actually witnessed, the man was reliving an experience as a new born baby. His body was sore and red and it felt unpleasant when he was first held by his mother; consequently he didn't want to be touched. Jesus was introduced into the situation. I didn't know it then, but this was nothing better than the psychotherapy derived from what Dave Hunt has called the "travelling specialists in inner healing and healing of the memories"* and which derive from "Christian" Primal Integration Therapy and from the "Primal Scream" methods of Arthur Janov. Indeed after first hearing about this ministry, and as a new Christian wanting all that the Lord had to give, I was eager to see what the experience might do for me.

At length a problem came up and it seemed right to arrange some of this ministry for myself. I did so with a mature Christian who was experienced in this area. Two

* "The Seduction of Christianity"

107

hours before the meeting was to begin, I believe the Lord spoke to me very clearly: "This ministry is not of Me". The "ministry" therefore did not take place. I waited on the Lord for more than two years, and after that time I was able to understand clearly what had been a witness in my spirit. I had worked out with my mind what God had prompted by His Spirit.

My constant prayer — one attached to the wall above my desk — was:

"Lord. Thank you for your Word. I am a believer not a doubter, but where I miss what you are saying, I pray you will protect me from error that would lead me astray."

I praise the Lord for honouring that prayer. What we are involved with in Inner Healing is more than just error. We are seeing person-to-person "Christian" ministry making use of the psychotherapies — mind power by another name — that proliferate in alternative medicine.*

Visualisation and Inner Healing

If there is one area that is very significant in the end-time deception, and yet which Christians are finding so difficult to understand, it is visualisation. I urge Christians to ask the Lord for this understanding. We wrestle against the authorities, against the powers of this dark world and against the spiritual forces of evil in the heavenly realm (Ephesians 6:12).

Visualisation is a very basic tool of operation in the occult realm and it has its foot very well into the Christian door. We have considered the subject previously but it is necessary to introduce it again here. It is a major technique of Inner Healing. It is valuable to look at visualisation again.

Inner Healing is just one — a most significant one — of the many therapies taken on by believers and Christianised by them as they came into the charismatic "renewal"

* For a closer look at the range of these therapies see "Understanding Alternative Medicine — Health Care in the New Age" by Roy Livesey (Marshall Morgan & Scott/New Wine Press — 1985)

wanting to "move with the Spirit" and bring wholeness, such as *they* had received, to *others*. Unfortunately they have set up ministries based upon psychology. That's all very well up to a point. Psychology has given us a clearer understanding of the unredeemed human character, but it fails to give biblical answers.

I do not pretend to bring any experience in Christian counselling, and I hesitate to come forward with easy alternatives to the visualisation methods of Inner Healing that are so unacceptable. There *are* great things to be achieved through good *scripturally-sound* counselling for the emotional areas. However I believe there are three areas that are worth remembering in the context of our analysis here:

Firstly, we all have to grow as Christians and the process of renewing the mind continues only as the subject wills. Also it takes time.

Secondly, with our will again, we can determine to do what has to be done. If we have received God's forgiveness and love, how can we withhold it from our earthly father, our grandfather, our grandmother, and all the rest that today's Inner Healers, almost inevitably come up with as keys to a seemingly difficult situation? We have to make a choice to forgive. The Inner Healer, though sincerely trying hard and believing himself to be hearing God, is almost invariably in the driving seat himself. For myself, one who has enjoyed good parental care and a very happy childhood, I also find difficulty in accepting the comparison of the earthly father to the heavenly Father in the way that the Inner Healers commonly do. Our heavenly God is far beyond such earthly comparison.

Thirdly, we can petition God; we can pray.

Prayer is the way through and God does meet the needs of the emotionally hurt. Counselling should help towards this goal, enabling the person in need to make the choice to forgive.

Satan has more than one way to promote the ultimate lie, that we can be like God and many in the churches have unknowingly come to believe it. Our walk with the Lord as

109

believers is a walk of faith. Believing is not the same thing as imagining or visualising, which are neither taught nor encouraged anywhere in Scripture. However visualisation is well understood by those familiar with the occult realm. It is a most powerful way of tuning in to the spirit world.

When we speak of visualising and imagining it must of course be acknowledged that there are non-occultic senses of these words. I believe it will be clear that what I write is not referring to these, nor is it referring to what the Lord can sovereignly do. Our reference is to Man's methods of influencing reality. It is one thing to visualise the sort of house we ask an architect to design or the garden we are planning. It is quite another to visualise all the seats in a church to be full when they are empty, or little men with hammers within the body attacking cancer cells. The ends may be in God's will, but the methods have to be His also. These are both real examples from my experience. If it suits his purpose Satan can bring a counterfeit healing but in any event our departure into fantasy (a misplaced faith) gives demons both the invitation and the opportunity.

And God saw that .... every imagination of the thoughts of his heart was only evil continually. (Genesis 6:5)

The truth of this scripture can be hard for many Christians to receive. Imagination and fantasy may well *seem* harmless enough, yet the Bible describes them as evil. Those who have had experience in witchcraft do not have the same difficulty. It has to be emphasised: visualisation is very dangerous.

Once again Hunt and McMahon's "The Seduction of Christianity" is an invaluable reference book for those who need to see how visualisation has become such a significant tool, and how it has come through from the occultists and so-called "thinkers" of the past to believers who are at the front in some of the "signs and wonders" ministries seen today. The report of one institute states that the use of the imagination is one of the most rapidly spreading new trends in psychology and education.

Materialisation also is known in the occult realm and

psychologists today are well into this sort of deception too. As one psychologist put it, if when we eat an apple and it becomes energy, or mind, it should not be difficult to grasp that the *thought* (or imagination) of an apple is capable of becoming an apple again — not an imagined apple but a real one. When we start to put faith in our imaginations, we are starting on a very slippery slope.

Jung was an occult psychiatrist and according to one teacher at the C.G. Jung Institute in the United States, visualisation or imagery is considered the most powerful tool in Jungian psychology for achieving direct contact with the unconscious and attaining "greater inner knowledge." This transpersonal psychology is the psychology of 'transcendent experience' and it is at this level of psychology that East meets West.

This transcendentalism gave rise to the "New Thought" which we have already seen in the idea that "thought", or the mind, controls all things. We see in the secular world the growth of interest in "Mind over Matter" pursuits such as karate and judo; parallel with this New Age activity, there is inside the Church a spirit tempting with the idea that God is not personal but a great *Mind* that can be activated through our own *minds*. The only answer is Jesus.

Fantasy, the Occult and the Counterfeiting of Jesus

What we do when we resort to fantasy situations is to separate ourselves from the real world and enter another where we unknowingly pretend as god over the scenes or situations we conjure up. Whether as children with fairy tales and fantasy games, as adults indulging in occult things, or as Christians visualising Jesus, we are not supposed to do it. We cannot rely on our imagination (Genesis 6:5) and, as Charles Finney warned, in every age men have fallen in love with fictions of their own imaginations over which they have stumbled into hell.*

When as a "searcher" in the occult realm, I attended a séance, the medium purported to bring me a message from the long-dead author of a book I had recently been reading. The title of that book was "The Life of Jesus". A demon can sometimes be on even surer ground in a fellowship of believing Christians where he can bring to someone a visualisation of Jesus! The Bible tells us that Satan can masquerade as an angel of light. It serves the purpose of demons extremely well to be mistaken for Jesus. The old witchdoctors would tell us that it doesn't matter what image is conjured up. The Christian position is a different one. We are not into *visualisation;* we are into *believing.* We all vary in our ability to visualise, some can do it easily, some cannot; but with God we can *all* believe. In "That Incredible Christian"** A.W. Tozer put it like this:

"Unwillingness to believe proves that men love darkness rather than light, while inability to visualise indicates no more than lack of imagination, something that will not be held against us at the judgment seat of Christ. The ability to visualise is found among vigorous-minded persons, whatever their moral or spiritual condition may be. A man with no faith in God or Christ may nevertheless have a keen imagination that enables him to picture inwardly anything he hears described .... another man who believes the Word of God implicitly and proves it by a life of obedience and charity may yet find it very hard to envisage the things he believes. Such a man is likely to blame himself for what he feels is unbelief. The wise Christian will not let his assurance depend upon his powers of imagination. True faith is not the intellectual ability to visualise unseen things to the satisfaction of our imperfect minds; it is rather the moral power to trust Christ ...."

The ideas that are invading Christianity are the same as those used extensively to motivate business success.

* "Crystal Christianity: A Guide to Personal Revival" by Charles G. Finney, ed David L. Young (Whitaker House — 1985)
** STL Publications, PO Box 48, Bromley, Kent.

Napoleon Hill, mentioned previously, is one who visualised great figures of history who put him in touch with infinite sources of wisdom. Hill's books are available in Christian bookshops throughout America. Satan has more than a single way of promoting the serpent's lie, subtly and not so subtly, among Christian believers. We should be beginning to see by now that his lie that we are as gods has not been without its success and that, spoken out clearly or subtly concealed, the message has been received in the minds of many Christian ministries.

Satan is at work in the Church. We need to understand that he is promoting the idea that we are as God and he is promoting the idea of the power there is in the mind (psychic power). Christians need to know their Bibles and to check out the teaching that they receive. Anchored in the Word of God, and with the discernment the Holy Spirit gives us personally, we can know the truth. The need is no less real whether we receive our teaching from our pastor or from an internationally renowned Bible teacher, whether we are reading Christian books or listening to teaching tapes. Surely it is sensible to check out the teaching we receive against what the Bible says. Surely also it is right to speak out against false Bible teaching, and if there is doubt then discussion is in order. It is not a matter of judging the teacher as many Christians will maintain, but it is right to evaluate all teaching, and to remember what the Bible teaches. It teaches that the Apostles spoke the names of men who were not teaching the Word of God correctly.

Of course the principle is the same whatever the size of a ministry, but let us remember that there are in these days some teachers whose televised broadcasts reach millions each week via satellite. Christian ministries in the United States are very often multi-million dollar businesses with an enormous audience, whether it be with tapes, books, conferences, radio, TV or whatever. Let us remember that we Christians are *all* part of the Body of Christ, and we need to look out for one another — to be watchmen.

The Root Takes us to a Jesuit: Teilhard de Chardin

Teilhard de Chardin has been described as the Father of the New Age. In her book "The Aquarian Conspiracy"* Marilyn Ferguson, herself a New Ager, tells us a survey showed that among New Agers, Teilhard de Chardin was the one most often quoted when asked whose New Age ideas most influenced them. It is interesting that a churchman, a Jesuit, should come top of her poll above C.G. Jung, Abraham Maslow, Aldous Huxley and J. Krishnamurti. Teilhard's name keeps cropping up as we look where false teaching in the Bible-believing church is coming from. His philosophy followed the lie of Genesis 3:5 and he saw Man merged with God. His ideas spawned the teaching of the Inner Healing that followed.

Dave Hunt and T.A. McMahon write** that perhaps no woman in this century has had a larger influence upon the Christianity of today than prolific best-selling author and teacher, Agnes Sanford. Quoted and recommended widely by Christian leaders, these established cult researchers tell us that Agnes Sanford was largely responsible for bringing visualisation and "healing of memories" into the church. They note that much of Agnes Sanford's writing is a clear reflection of Teilhardian philosophy. In her book, "The Healing Gifts of the Spirit", she tells us that God is the very "life force" existing in a radiation of an energy from which all things evolved, and that God is *in* the flowers and *in* the birds. Such teaching is more Hindu than Christian. In "The Healing Gifts of the Spirit" Agnes Sanford recognises that we need Jesus' life and teachings; strangely she believes He tried raising people by His teachings alone and this did not work. She believed our Lord's principles were right and that God's love was blacked out from Man by what she called the negative thought vibrations. She believed that in the

* "The Aquarian Conspiracy" 1980 (Granada 1982)
** "The Seduction of Christianity"

114

atonement Jesus lowered His *thought vibrations* of humanity and received into Himself Man's *thoughts* of sin, sickness, pain and death. In another place she describes, how she could control the will of her children, and how, after a few months of practice she could influence her children by remote control. It is this root of imagination, visualisation and straight-forward witchcraft that continues through the ministers who followed on from her.

The Bible says, *Thou will keep him in perfect peace, whose mind is stayed on thee: because he trusteth in thee.*

(Isaiah 26:3)

Isaiah doesn't speak of an *open* mind or a passive mind. Indeed anyone who knows the ways of the occult, knows the danger of the open mind and the metaphysical methods to which Agnes Sanford refers. Far from being even just a risk, I believe the danger is inevitable. The metaphysical is the demonic supernatural, and it is hard to imagine how the ideas of such a lady did not disqualify her from receiving the Christian support that she enjoyed. I suppose the answer then is the same answer to explain the following of many today — "signs and wonders". "Does Inner Healing work?": that is *not* the question.

Inner Healing certainly can "work". There is no doubt about that. "Where does the power come from?": *That is the question for today.*

A Roman Catholic calls up Mary

Many have picked up the wrong Sanford teaching and in the well-known ministry of one who started off as a Roman Catholic priest, we see that he follows the now familiar pattern of recreating the past and visualising Jesus walking back through it. The argument runs that Jesus is not in the time dimension. However the fact is that true healing comes by believing God and not by an unknowing invitation to demons brought about by visualisation. It may well be that the motive and intention is good. Yet, as we have considered previously, demons will assuredly take advantage where the word of God allows and where the conditions are met. We need not lack the knowledge that is available in the Word. This is not to say the Lord will never show mercy and protect us, but He can teach us by our mistakes and as we turn from disobedience to obedience.

There is no foundation in Scripture for the idea that we can ask Jesus to walk back to the time we were hurt to free us from the effects of that wound in the present. Jesus can prompt our spirit as to the past, but He can't be manipulated to walk back in time. He can simply point us to his Word.

I believe Christians need to become generally more aware that exposure to any unscriptural healing techniques can bring them into bondage that will need to be broken by renunciation and repentance just like any other occult sin.

An extra injection of idolatry is brought into this example from the minister's background as a Roman Catholic priest. In one book, he adds this Roman flavour and states that if the person missed out on a mother's love in any way he can ask Jesus (if the person is a Catholic) to send His mother Mary to do what mothers do to provide children with love and security. I believe it is relevant to note that Inner Healers teaching the "visualisation" message are generally not very concerned about the accuracy of the picture that is visualised or called upon. This man, well regarded by his fellow Inner Healers, calls up Mary.

Another Leading Lady Takes the Stage

"The Gift of Inner Healing" by Ruth Carter Stapleton was one of the first Christian books to come into my possession after I was born again. The cover of the book describes her as a Christian counsellor who has brought healing to thousands and who is sharing with her readers "a new approach to mankind's hurts and wrong attitudes."*

An example Mrs Stapleton gives in one of her books is

* "The Gift of Inner Healing" by Ruth Carter Stapleton (Word, Inc. Waco TX 1976) Hodder & Stoughton — 1977)

useful to identify the inner healing therapy, albeit her ministry is essentially little different from the rest who have picked up on Agnes Sanford's teaching.

Ruth, the sister of Jimmy Carter the former American President who accordingly attracted much attention to herself and to the "born again" idea in America, gives us this example. She tells of a young woman who became involved in drugs and crime because of the "self-loathing" she felt at being an illegitimate child. Ruth took her back in a "guided meditation" in which Christ was visualised as present during the act of fornication that caused her conception. The idea, it seems, was to make it "holy and pure, an act of God .... ordained by her heavenly Father." Where is the Scripture that allows for Jesus journeying back into the past? Like so much in the occult, the method will appear to work, but the way of the real Jesus is a much better way. Is it not better that we search our hearts with the help of the Holy Spirit so that we may confess all the sin He brings to mind, meet all the conditions, and receive the healing and work out our salvation? Certainly we seek a wholeness that includes inner healing. What we don't want are the occult techniques and methods which so easily creep in when we focus on "signs and wonders" and healings instead of on Jesus, the Word.

"We love and forgive others because of God's love and forgiveness to us. It is that simple. This is the 'fruit of the Spirit' that results from Christ living in us. If we are willing to face this truth, then He will give us the strength to carry it out. Inner Healing is based upon a denial that this is all we need; 'something more' must be involved, and that 'something' is borrowed from a variety of psychotherapies, most of which are related to shamanism."*

With Ruth, as for many like her, we can examine what is said to an audience of people belonging to a cult, and who readily accept the message, in order to see the teacher's error more clearly. Unbelievers with "healing" ministries

* "The Seduction of Christianity"

are quite well able to introduce a measure of Christian language in a presentation to a church audience and so deceive all but the discerning, and perhaps in a reverse sense Ruth was able to make herself more clear to Christians when speaking at a meeting of the Unity School of Christianity. Unity is a religious cult similar to Christian Science and the Atonement to them is a reuniting of our consciousness with the God-consciousness within, making us again ''at-one'' (atonement) with God. Whatever the play on words the origin is found in Hinduism where all are gods. Speaking before a Unity congregation in Chicago in 1978 this controversial lady perhaps sensed she was on friendly ground: ''If there are any of you right now who are having pain within your body, God is wholeness, and You are God. In you He lives and moves and has His being. So let His wholeness express Himself in you right now. Claim His wholeness within your bodies right now.''*

Visualisation techniques are rooted in the occult. They are designed by the powers of darkness to bring us to the place that Eve was brought to in Genesis 3:5: *''Ye shall be as gods.''* It appears Ruth was brought to that place: ''.... God is wholeness, and You are God.''

Today's Inner Healers: The Same Counterfeit Spirit

Teilhard de Chardin, Agnes Sanford and Ruth Carter Stapleton are no longer alive. When I have presented what they believed to some of today's Christian Inner Healers they have claimed to recognise what seem to them to be the excesses of these predecessors. Rather I believe the truth is that today there are those like Ruth who have been brought to the place where they would (given the right audience at least) *declare* their godhood. Ruth has said to her audience ''.... and you are God'' just as I heard my ''favourite Faith

* From ''Ruth'' by Brooks Alexander. Reprinted by permission of Spiritual Counterfeits Project, Inc. © 1980 (''Inner Healing Issue'' — S.C.P. Journal April 1980)

118

teacher'' say: ''You don't have a god in you; you are one.''
No matter what these leaders are led or are not led to spell
out before certain audiences, let us recognise the spiritual
war and discern the *spirit* that is at work in Inner Healing.

Visualising the Kingdom

It has already been stated that one of Satan's purposes seems
to be to plant the idea of Christ's reign *in us, on earth* —
a reign *through* the corporate body of believers. We examine
further the doctrine of the Manifest Sons of God in chapter
twelve.

There abounds the idea that we need to see the individual
healed and made whole, fit to rule before the personal return
of Jesus Christ, not *in the air* but *on the ground* to rule over
the Kingdom *we* are to establish for Him. We are to be
perfected, and it is argued, the Kingdom will be brought to
perfection too — ready for Jesus to come. Visualisation, a
much used tool in Inner Healing, has its place in bringing
in the Kingdom too! When in America I was able to acquire
a copy of ''The Secret Kingdom'' by top Christian TV
director, Pat Robertson. In it, Robertson, a possible U.S.
Presidential contender, shows that if the Kingdom is to be
implemented on earth now we shall need to be involved in
its visualisation!

In a chapter note of ''A Planned Deception'', Constance
Cumbey writes this of Pat Robertson, Founder of Christian
Broadcasting Network (CBN): ''According to a CBN movie
'For I have Chosen You' the prophecy that God chose CBN
and Pat Robertson to 'usher in the coming of my Son' came
through Harold Bredesen. This took place at a prayer
meeting. In a closed circuit telethon in the fall of 1982, Pat
Robertson solicited donations for his television station in the
Middle East. He told the audience he was doing so because
Jesus had appeared to him in a vision and told him that he
(Robertson) had been appointed a modern day John the
Baptist to usher in His coming. Further, he says Jesus said
he wanted Pat Robertson to get the first television shots of

his return to earth. Surely this scenario does not fit Scripture. .... My understanding of the prophecy is that Jesus is returning IN the air — not ON the air!"*

Every eye shall see Him.   (Revelation 1:7).

There is no more place for mind power methods in the *Church* than there is in medicine for occult alternative therapies which increasingly supplant the legitimate medicine provided for *Man* by the Bible and science. Likewise there is no more place for mind power methods in **building the Church** (or the "Kingdom"!) than there is for "inner healing techniques", prosperity and the other so-called needs of *Man* introduced into the Church to increasingly supplant the ways that God has laid down. We examine further false ideas about the "Kingdom" in chapters thirteen and fourteen.

* Published by Pointe Publishers, Inc. 22317 Kelly Road, East Detroit, Michigan 48021 (1985)

8
Signs and Wonders

The Bible tells us that the Antichrist will come *"after the working of Satan with all power and signs and lying wonders"* (2 Thessalonians 2:9). It is true that we have a wonder-working God who is the same yesterday, today and forever. We do see God's miracles today but we do also see Satan's counterfeit. We in the Body of Christ need the Holy Spirit's discernment as well as His miracles, because counterfeit signs and wonders will increase.

"Signs and Wonders" and no Discernment

The "signs and wonders" ministry from America and referred to previously is making a big impact on the Church in Britain at this time.

I believe the focus is *intended* to be only on Jesus — but what of the emphasis on signs and wonders? It is not surprising that many have attended these teaching meetings looking for new insights on how to get Jesus' supernatural working in their ministries. However there is a real danger that many, whether they have experienced the supernatural in their own lives and ministries or not, can find themselves taking their eyes off Jesus as they look to the supernatural for their healings and miracles.

We see so much sickness that the longing for God's supernatural power to manifest in the situation is understandable. But it is easy to take our eyes off Jesus, and when we do so in this area of the supernatural, there can be a price to pay. Surely Satan likes nothing more than to counterfeit the miracles of Jesus! Pharaoh's magicians did the same signs as Moses, and the Devil would love to bring biblical healing into disrepute.

We need to understand that Satan's army marshalled in the spiritual realm can counterfeit miracles for some who, in the name of Jesus, are merely mouthing words in an intellectual way and apart from a leading of the Holy Spirit. This is not co-operation with the God who heals. Also what of those in these teaching groups who don't *know* Jesus?

Not every one that saith unto me, Lord, Lord, shall enter into the kingdom of heaven; but he that doeth the will of my Father which is in heaven.

Many will say to me in that day, Lord, Lord, have we not prophesied in thy name? and in thy name have cast out devils? and in thy name done many wonderful works?

And then will I profess unto them, I never knew you: depart from me, ye that work iniquity.

(Matthew 7:21—23)

It is a real danger in teaching "signs and wonders" that whilst the teaching may be good, the class or congregation, big or small, with new or with mature believers, may be unable to receive it. Others may not even *know* Jesus. Surely there are leaders and teachers who do not recognise those who don't *know* Jesus; the job is made more difficult by what is really a new 'form of godliness'. This can take the form of impressive "praise and worship", tongues and manifestation of various "gifts" by those who simply have no fruits. It is by their fruits we shall know them. Do they even *know* Jesus? There is a real need for discernment.

The teaching materials of the one "Signs and Wonders" teacher I believe God has constantly brought to my attention show a lack of discernment. Many who *do* know very well that demons *can* counterfeit physical healing (even though they put something much worse than the original sickness in its place) often have little discernment when demonic activity comes into a *Christian* fellowship. Discernment is greatly needed in the body of Christ in these days when the Holy Spirit is at work.

122

Occult activity is increasing too; it surely must according to Scripture and if it is to sustain Antichrist who will come in the flesh. Teaching that encourages signs and wonders *must* include more than a passing reference to discernment. In the teaching materials I have, I not only find the absence of teaching on discernment, but an evident lack of it in the materials themselves. In the examples of signs and wonders ministries since the early Church we read profiles of some of the "major household names" in church history. We are encouraged to observe for ourselves that the moving of the Holy Spirit in signs and wonders has not ceased since the early church.

One of those profiled was Ignatius de Loyola. Sandwiched between Martin Luther (1483—1546) who slightly pre-dated Loyola, and John Calvin (1509—1564) who slightly post-dated him, these three men presented examples from one of the three major historical periods — "The patristic, medieval and reformation-modern". Luther and Calvin need no introduction to Christians today; they were the reformers who pulled the Protestants back from Rome. Who then was Ignatius de Loyola?

Loyola's "Spiritual Exercises"

Loyola was the Founder of the Society of Jesus (the Jesuits). He became Rome's answer to Luther's Reformation, replacing the Inquisition with a perhaps more formidable and subtle, if less bloody approach. What then was Loyola's gift to the Jesuits; what was his secret? Boehmer was a professor at the University of Bonn and he wrote: "Ignatius de Loyola understood more clearly than any other leader of men who preceded him that the best way to raise a man to a certain ideal is to become master of his imagination. We 'imbue into him spiritual forces which he would find very difficult to eliminate later', forces more lasting than all the best principles and doctrines; these forces can come up again to the surface, sometimes after years of not even mentioning them, and become so imperative that the will finds itself unable to oppose any obstacle, and has to follow their irresistible impulse."*

It is true that Rome made Loyola a "Saint". "Understanding the New Age"** includes a look at the counterfeit church which is in Rome and at Jesuit-power which is such a significant part of it. What we are concerned with here is *counterfeit* signs and wonders. During the time of his ascetic life in the monastery Loyola developed what became known as "The Spiritual Exercises." These involved methods of "praying" in conjunction with breathing exercises in a strictly controlled way under the supervision of a Director. It was a way to gain control of the minds of others.

The Spiritual Exercises did not die out with Ignatius de Loyola. Books dealing with them can be found in some Christian bookshops and I received in my mail recently a brochure inviting my consideration of a Jesuit-run three month residential course "making the full spiritual exercises of St. Ignatius." I read that the exercises had received the approval of successive Popes and that they have been the starting point for most forms of spiritual retreat in the Christian world since the sixteenth century. Central to both spiritual direction and counselling was what the brochure called an "active listening." An essential prerequisite in making the spiritual exercises was to be "in touch with one's own experience."

The brochure described the position very correctly, and in "The Contemplative Way of Prayer: Deepening Your Life with God",*** Robert Faricy, a Jesuit priest, and Lucy Rooney remind us of the Roman Catholic understanding of baptism in the Spirit. The authors add that some have received such a grace when following the exercises of Ignatius de Loyola.

Loyola will have experienced many "signs and wonders". Those following him today, receiving a counterfeit experience, will be open to "signs and wonders" too. What

* "Les Jesuites" by H. Boehmer (Armand Colin, Paris 1910)
** "Understanding the New Age" by Roy Livesey (New Wine Press — 1986)
*** Published by Servant Publications, Ann Arbor, Michigan — 1986

Christians need to be able to do is to discern the counterfeit, separating it from the genuine work of the Holy Spirit.

In this section we do not look at the Charismatic Movement and Rome's infiltration of it; we see that in chapter ten. What we see here, effected through the "Spiritual Exercises", is the formal and organised inducement of passivity; it is the groundwork, the "opening up" for "signs and wonders" (counterfeit not genuine) and the infiltration of the charismatic Christian scene bringing confusion with the ministries of those truly moving in the power of God.

A Church of England Training Day for Lay Readers

One Lay-reader in training rang me from the north of England after his extraordinary "training-day" had been concluded. He had recognised the "Spiritual Exercises" which were being taught and encouraged. Approximately one hundred were present. They were Lay-readers, Lay-readers in training, and Lay-assistants from one diocese of the Church of England.

A Church of England minister, a priest of the Anglo-Catholic tradition, led their time together introducing the assembly to the writing of Jesuit priest, Anthony De Mello.

The exercises, whch were termed an exercise in silence, were led in the following order:

1. "Close your eyes for two minutes, think on common feelings which you normally do not notice, feelings like the touch of your clothes upon your body, your feet in your shoes, the touch of your hands, the atmosphere on your face ...."
2. After opening the eyes the next session lasted five minutes. The first two minutes were for emptying the mind and the remainder of the time was to enjoy whatever entered into the mind.

3. Next, it was time to share "feelings and failures" with those around. It was expected that many would have been unable to fully put off interruptions which came into the mind. However success would come by working at it.
4. The next session took the form of uttering the "divine name" of "Jesus". The idea was following the tradition of the Orthodox Church (Greek and Russian), inhaling, then exhaling and saying the name of Jesus while exhaling. "Inhale then exhale (Je...sus); inhale then exhale (Je...sus); inhale then exhale (Je...sus) .... and so on."
5. The session led onto a repeating of the words: "Lord have mercy; Lord have mercy; Lord have mercy .... and so on."
6. After another break to "talk and reflect" the final session began. This time the purpose was to focus (with closed eyes) upon oneself, to get to know oneself.

That is how my friend described it. Of course what we see here is an introduction to psychic power, to mind power. The precise form adopted can vary, yet there is enough in the six steps above to make the process at once recognisable to those with occult experience. Some of those present will have declared at the end of the day that the whole exercise was "barmy"; in other words nothing will have seemed to work for them. Others, more and more in these days having already been opened up by previous occult experience, will reflect on the benefit they "felt" from the day. A third group, a very small minority, including my friend, will have discerned what was really going on; they will have recognised the spiritual forces which were at work. Yet all can be affected by involvement with such practices whatever their motive.

What those hundred or so men and women of good motive were being introduced to were Jesuit Spiritual Exercises. They were being introduced to *"the vain repetitions, as the heathen do"* (Matthew 6:7). They were being introduced to the supernatural.

Loyola Profiled in Christian Teaching Materials

It was against the background of my own occult experience and familiarity with the sort of exercises enumerated above that I viewed with horror the sight of the name of Ignatius de Loyola profiled in the teaching materials of a "Signs and Wonders" teacher.

What can be the purpose of including such profiles in Christian teaching materials without mention of the need for discernment? What can be the purpose of including Loyola? Was that the Holy Spirit moving in signs and wonders? The miracle cures of Lourdes in France are profiled too. Among the many Roman Catholics profiled we see the recommend-ation of a pair of Jesuit priests; we are told they are highly trained in psychology and combine the best insights in this field with their theological understanding which is shaped by charismatic experience. In their own book, these two, prominent in the inner healing movement, demonstrate the usual psychological techniques of imagining Jesus, and Mary also! I was reminded of the ministry of "Healing of Memories" where the result can be the same whether the recall is from childhood, from the time in the womb, or from a past life. The work of the inner healers, whether Christian or not, seems to be as effective whether the job is done by a conjured Jesus, Mary or indeed the visualisation of any other personality.

However soundly based a "Signs and Wonders" teaching ministry might be in other respects, there are great dangers without discernment. Generally what we have been looking at in this book are Man's attempts — in some cases with Satan's help — to build a system on techniques that have been known to occultists for thousands of years.

Science and Medicine

Many of us are being deceived by much that is disguised as science, but which is not science at all. It is true that what can be explained scientifically cannot be supernatural whether in God's realm or in Satan's. However science has moved a long way since the law of gravity was discovered. Like so much else in these days science is extraordinarily complex. Even over a very few years science has made great advances. These have involved co-operation between scientists. They rely on each others' results and this search for knowledge has taken Man further from God. Science, sound enough in itself, has been the vehicle for the sort of deception that discerning Christians have seen writ large in psychology. Man has left himself open to lying signs and wonders (2 Thessalonians 2:9).

Perhaps nowhere can the deceptions brought to science be better seen than in the area of medicine. Here the main focus is on "Does it work?" rather than "Where does the power come from?" The fact is, doctors *always* got results. They got them through the faith the patient places in the doctor. Then the results came from drugs. Now, more and more, the results are through alternative therapies with an occult spiritual base. Modern man puts it all down to science — the inert placebos and concoctions which have for so long been provided by medicine, the devastating hallucinatory, addictive or hypnotic drugs of today, and the growing number of seemingly innocuous therapies rooted in the occult.

When we don't look to the Bible for our healing provision we shall inevitably remain a target for the deceptions Satan has for us. The area of health and healing is one in which Satan is very active in these days. The pharmaceutical industry has provided the drugs. Doctors have prescribed them. Now patients, reacting against them, are ready to be directed to therapies that are really occult.

Alternative Medicine

Satan has invaded medicine and he has invaded the church. We cannot ignore the spiritual status of those who seek to bring healing in either place. This has been much evidenced to me from the response I have had since the publication of "Understanding Alternative Medicine". I have received numerous pleas from those to whom God has given discernment: "What do I *do* about my pastor who is directing people to this or that therapist?" These therapists are sometimes leaders in the pastor's own fellowhip! The reaction to drugs has brought a boom in the business of alternative medicine. The Beatles moved from drugs to TM, but like many today they were moving on in the spiritual realm.

Bio-kinesiology was one that was recommended. It is difficult to imagine a more bizarre therapy, and it is a sign of the-end-times when believers are being taken in by treatments such as this. The particular therapy is described in "Understanding Alternative Medicine" and the example described to one Christian medical practitioner, and related to me, is as follows:

The idea is to identify dietary substances which would be harmful to the patient. Small amounts of the substance under test are in turn placed upon the subject's tongue whilst the practitioner attempts to lower the subject's arm extended first above the head, then about waist level, and then lower. Apparently it is quite easy for the subject to resist these attempts to move his arm, except when any dietary substance "harmful" to him is placed upon his tongue when he seems powerless to resist the force applied by the practitioner.

Then a similar procedure is repeated, but this time instead of the substances being placed on the tongue they remain in their unopened bottle and the bottle is placed on the skin of the abdomen. If this has the same apparent effect on muscle power, then the harmful substances are thus identified.

Neurologists properly tell us that muscle power in the same individual will vary and depend most of all on his *will* to resist. It is also true that we have the deception of that common denominator found in so much of the paranormal — "energy". The word biokinesiology is derived from "kinetic" (energy; Gk "kinetikos") but it is a counterfeit; for it to be otherwise, and as one Christian writer* has put it, it seems every text-book on physiology would have to be re-written.

In another example a lady, by any view a mature Christian, was told to "submit with humility" by her pastor. One of the conditions was that under no circumstances was she ever to mention *Reflexology* or her views concerning it. That is in a go-ahead church of nearly one thousand members. My correspondent was concerned at the active promotion of Reflexology in her fellowship and at the practice of the therapy by one of the church leaders.

What is Reflexology? It's "Signs and Wonders" again. But it's not Christian. It is from the father of lies.

"Reflexology is traceable back to China five thousand years ago. It was also known in ancient Egypt. Practitioners believe there are ten energy channels, each covering all the organs in a zone of the body. By feeling the feet they believe they can find which channel is blocked; then they massage the feet seeking to restore the energy flow. I have studied and done this myself. There has perhaps been little detailed research into the origins, and beyond what millions are reading in modern-day "alternative health" guides. There is enough for the discerning Christian!"**

A central idea in both reflexology and biokinesiology is that of energy channels. This idea of "energy", of "life force", crops up again and again in the occult and by those who will deny God. We meet it again in homoeopathy, the flagship that leads the "holistic" deception among Christians. We take a special look at this therapy in the next chapter.

In the past scientists could never make head nor tail of these

---

* "The Holistic Healers" by Reisser, Reisser and Weldon (Inter Varsity Press — USA, 1983)
** "Understanding Alternative Medicine" by Roy Livesey (Marshall, Morgan & Scott/Life Changing Books & New Wine Press, 1985)

energies. They didn't exist as far as they were concerned. They don't exist today, but some scientists' *minds* are being changed, not by learning but by mind control techniques. More and more are coming up with answers that are only available through the influence of demons. If Christians themselves knew a little more about the character of demons and the nature of spiritual warfare, fewer would be taken in by the many deceptions provided in the name of science in these days. The spirit of Antichrist surely exists in the area of so-called science today. When he comes in the flesh isn't it inconceivable that he won't *use* the "science" which has been made ready for him?

Signs and Wonders are Real Enough Whether from God or the Devil

One of my early conversations as a young Christian was with a mature brother in Christ who viewed counterfeit signs and wonders as being something in the nature of a conjuring trick. The fact is that signs and wonders are real whether worked in the power of the Holy Spirit through us or worked by the master counterfeiter who seeks to copy all that God does.

Reflexology can work. Bio-kinesiology can work. During a training course when a searcher in the occult realm I learned, and in class practised, reflexology. Bear in mind it needn't take a long and involved training when we are truly submitted. It matters little to the powers of darkness if a reflexology student doesn't *exactly* find one of the thousands of different supposed points on the foot to bring relief to a shoulder or to diagnose a backache. It matters little to them if the acupuncturist with his heart in the right place puts his needles in the wrong place; the so-called energy channels are anyway in different places for the reflexologist, the acupuncturist and all the rest who are seeking to balance up our body "energies" in these days.

My own introduction to alternative medicine, described

more fully in "New Age to New Birth",* came as the result of signs and wonders witnessed on public platforms and at séances whilst I was dangerously and very misguidedly investigating the world of the psychics and spiritualists. At the time I didn't know it was forbidden by God (Deuteronomy 18:10). During the course of that "search" I witnessed many healings and "Signs and Wonders", I attended "Healing" services in what just *happened* to be Anglican churches and where the invited minister was a known spiritualist, and most significantly I was miraculously healed of a complaint I had suffered for eighteen years. Twice a day for the previous eight years I had received treatment. It is in the light of that experience, on the top of what the Bible so clearly warns, that my heart has so often grieved as I have watched the increasing focus on "Signs and Wonders" in the Church. It is true the Holy Spirit is moving today. My own salvation and that of so many around me is evidence enough, but nearly everywhere I see Christians going after every wind of doctrine; they want to get results and they go were the "signs and wonders" are. If it works, it's good! If there are results from this or that method, it's good!

The purpose of this book is to bring a different question into the minds of Christians. That question is: "Which Spirit?" Which spirit is at work; is it the Holy Spirit? I believe that as we *love* the truth (2 Thessalonians 2:10) and ask God for the discernment we need, then He will give discernment to us.

Tingling Hands!

I was able to take the opportunity to witness the ministry of the "Signs and Wonders" teacher, referred to previously, at first hand at a gathering of seven or eight thousand at a European convention. In my notebook I recorded just a few of this minister's words to confirm the alarm bells already ringing in my spirit. At one point when several

* "New Age to New Birth — A Personal Testimony of Two Kingdoms" (New Wine Press) — 1986

hundred were standing and awaiting to be prayed for, the general invitation was made: "If you feel tingling or heat — energy — in your hands I want you to touch one who is standing." I knew the tingling proved nothing; I met it in the occult. Of course there was much that was scriptural and a great deal that was good. What we had was a *mixture* as regards the ministry and I thought of rotten apples in a barrel. Also with such a large audience, itself inevitably a mixture of the saved, unsaved and those having varying degrees of spiritual discernment, the *barrel* was a very big one!

How many spiritualists are there with tingling hands in any crowd of eight thousand? As a full-time "searcher" in the occult realm I believe I would have made sure and attended, attracted by the "signs and wonders". Whatever the heart of those on the platform, the peering eyes of many in the enormous gathering clearly evidenced where *their* focus was. Those ministering were asked to *focus* on the "person who needs the touch." Surely there was much *focus* on Signs and Wonders! Certainly the name of Jesus was lifted up and intentions were sincere. It is true also that some were discerning and for each session God wonderfully undertook to set me down alongside such a person. I believe good and bad will be manifest from the spirits at work, but like the apples in the barrel, and unless we attend to discernment based upon what the Bible says and what the Holy Spirit will give, it may be expected that in time more fruit will turn bad. The only answer for believers is that they exercise real discernment and of course the emphasis must be on *Jesus*.

Many in that vast gathering were from the "liberal" and Roman Catholic churches. They had come into "renewal". We can thank God for those who are reaching out to the Lord in those places. Now, renewed by the Spirit, the need is discernment.

"Liberal Church" to "Renewed Church": Discernment Urgently Needed!

It was noted in chapter three, as Watchman Nee has written, that Man with his focus on the things of the world, has nothing to fear from the dangers of passivity. Such dangers are not present in the "liberal" churches that proliferate in our time.

Paul writes to Timothy in the Second Epistle of the dangerous times in the last days. Certainly at the start of chapter four we saw a clear description of where liberalism and modern theology has led. Paul describes it as *"having a form of godliness, but denying the power thereof"* (2 Timothy 3:5). Whilst we do not look in detail at this liberalism — most Christians now easily recognise the Bishops and leaders of what has been called churchianity — it needs to be stated that the professing Church, which has long since ceased to "endure sound doctrine", remains still a subtle threat to the growth of real Christianity. Indeed we can join Walter Martin, referred to previously, and fairly speak of the *Cult* of Liberalism, and it is especially dangerous because it infests and infiltrates the true Church without coming out into the open with what it believes. Satan does seem to have taken much ground in the denominations; this is seen by looking at those there who are in authority.

Today the enemy initiatives have shifted and the emphasis in this book is to focus on the error that has attached itself to the "Renewal" of recent years. I believe that Paul's words are appropriate for the Church today just as they were when *liberalism* first established itself.

> *Preach the word; be instant in season, out of season; reprove, rebuke, exhort with all longsuffering and doctrine.*
>
> *For the time will come when they will not endure sound doctrine; but after their own lusts shall they heap to themselves teachers, having itching ears;*
>
> *And they shall turn away their ears from the truth, and shall be turned unto fables.* (2 Timothy 4:2—4)

Whether it be the cult of Liberal Theology or the cult of Self-Esteem, whether it be the error or the lack of discernment that invades through Positive Confession or through focusing on Signs and Wonders, whether it be the focus on ourselves and what *we* or our *leaders* can do through visualisation, inner healing, shepherding groups or whatever, what is needed in the Church has been well provided for in the Word of God.

Now with renewed spirits, those newly established in Christ need to have their minds renewed by the Word of God. They need defences, they need to put on the armour of God, and be equipped to withstand the passivity and experiences encouraged by the ''signs and wonders'' gatherings such as previously described. Given the new spiritual state, including the enthusiasm for the things of God, Satan has a new strategy. It is a strategy that gets our focus on experiences, and eventually on experiences that he will mostly provide.

We need leaders who will *''preach the word; be instant in season; reprove, rebuke, exhort with all longsuffering and doctrine''* (2 Timothy 4:2). This was Paul's charge to Timothy, he was to preach Jesus, and in these last days it applies not just to those fallen to ''liberalism'' but also to those in ''renewal'' still in their churches and to those in fellowships of born-again believers.

Yet so successful has the enemy been, many of the teachers in their sincerity and innocence have already been led astray. Even so, every answer is in the Word. As we love the truth and check teaching against the Word as the Bible tells us (Acts 17:11), we can be kept safe.

9

Homoeopathy — Flagship of "Holistic" Deception

Christians who get sick and who are not tempted by any of the deceptions thus far described are given a further opportunity. They can turn to one of the holistic health treatments that are available. This is an area also described as alternative medicine.

Conscious of the dangers inherent in many medical treatments and understandably refusing to suffer the side-effects of all kinds of addictive, hallucinatory and hypnotic drugs, more and more Christians are turning to what they see as natural remedies with no concomitant side-effect or danger. While they are for the most part undiscerning, they do not find it strange that the other main group flocking to these thereapies comprises the New Agers. It is the New Agers in their focus on the creation who not only support the growing trade but who in a large measure provide the people who introduce and promote the new therapies in all their various forms and varieties.

The problem once again, as we have seen with the Inner Healing and the Signs and Wonders, the Positive Confession and the other mind-based "Name It and Claim It" deceptions, is that things are not what they seem. More and more as the supernatural becomes increasingly commonplace we have to take care to distinguish it from the natural. Indeed it is a sign of the end-time that science is so combining with the occult and with non-Christian religion that there is needed an even greater caution with what science provides and with the explanations that scientists give us.

It is surely a sign of the end-time deception about which the Bible speaks when therapies like homoeopathy see a growth of support from Christians. It is true that many are hearing the Lord and are repenting of their involvement with it. However for Christians, homoeopathy, always the most "respectable" of them, is truly the flagship of the Alternative Medicine armada.

Homoeopathy was given to its founder Hahnemann in the last century by what he believed was a divine revelation. This foundation rests on the strange idea that highly diluted solutions based upon herbs or minerals are more powerful as the dilution is greater. The power is believed to depend on shaking to release the energy from the herb or mineral into the water. However no serious scientific support for that idea can be found. Rather there is a spiritual doctrine and Hahnemann's disciples are encouraged to meditate on the "Organ of the Art of Healing". This is the ancient "Bible" of the homoeopaths and they are encouraged to grasp the "spirit" of it.

The President of the International League on Homoeopathy, a doctor from Rome, at the Montreaux International Congress for the 150th Anniversary in 1960, chose words which should speak to the discerning Christian:
"It's futile to reject this or that principle enunciated in the 'Organ'. There remains more than enough to recognise the unfathomable intuition and divinatory spirit of its author."*

My book, "Beware Alternative Medicine", published in 1983, was, as far as I am aware the first Christian book in the English language which stated unequivocally that homoeopathy was from deceiving spirits and was occult. I relate that only to evidence the grip that Satan has had, and the measure of the deception there has been since homoeopathy arrived in Britain around 1840. This is all the more remarkable given the extraordinary things witnessed in homoeopathy by the well-qualified and highly educated people who head up the homoeopathy fraternity in Britain.

* Swiss Homoeopathic Journal No.4/1960

As an example of the extraordinary deception, homoeopaths often continue the process of diluting and shaking long after the point where the scientist declares there to be no longer any possibility that even a single molecule of the original substance remains in the solution. In other words pure water is diluted with pure water!

Yet as Christians we need to understand why homoeopathy, and indeed many other seemingly ridiculous treatments, are not discounted or abandoned. The reason is simple. They work!

Certainly there can be a measure of mind-power and placebo effect but what we have is magic. The deceiver as ever has begun with something good. The Bible says: *"the fruit thereof shall be for meat, and the leaf thereof for medicine"* (Ezekiel 47:12). Satan begins with the leaf, the herb, and he is so effective that even after it is completely diluted out and a ritual magic shaking substituted in its place, the undiscerning are quite satisfied to receive what are seen as the benefits.

Indeed there are no benefits from homoeopathy. HOMOEOPATHY IS DANGEROUS. Against the physical and emotional reliefs that can result, there is always a very high price to be paid.

A Cautionary Word About All Testimonies

Whilst writing this book and endeavouring to take a great deal of care with scriptures, checking and rechecking manuscripts with those who know their Bibles well, I do not escape the fact that I am not a Bible scholar myself. The danger of such a position can be the tendency to rely excessively on what is commonly called testimony and what might more helpfully be decribed as experiences. I have known that trap; apart from an understanding of the Word of God, it is all too easy to major on testimony — on experiences.

I do not relate here my own testimony of how I first came to the belief that homoeopathy is occult. Firstly, it was given at length in "Understanding Alternative Medicine". It began with a clear intuition, quite apart from any understanding or immediate confirmation from the Word of God; but it is better to bring the focus, seen in this chapter, on what homoeopathy is, what it involves, and what the Bible says, rather than on the peculiarly individual ways by which we are each brought to the place where we can see reality. In another testimony which follows we see an example of how one practitioner came to see the deception in homoeopathy, but there is no substitute for knowing what homoeopathy is, for knowing its roots, and for knowing what the Bible says about it.

On that basis, and whatever our intellectual level, if we are not deceived (often by involvement with these things), we will easily see the stupidity of the homoeopathic idea. We have to look to Jesus; no testimony, and certainly not my own, can be reckoned for its own merits; that is the case where testimonies of discernment, including of homoeopathy, are concerned. The value of my homoeopathy testimony came as I checked out with my understanding what God seemed to be saying. Testimonies, like experiences, are not something to look for; once we take our eyes off Jesus and set them on testimonies it can be open to the deceiver to make good our desires. Rather it is when we look back — Bible in hand — that we can marvel at God's grace and at the lengths He has gone to, in spite of all our disobedience and misunderstandings, to bring us closer to Him.

Some Christians have started to become aware of what is seen as the "homoeopathy controversy". The debate was helped along in 1985 when the magazine "Christian Woman" devoted a large section to homoeopathy. There were two contributors; one was "for" and one "against". Writing her case in favour of homoeopathy was homoeo-pathic practitioner and Christian alternative medicine clinic principal, Pearl Coleman.

More than two years after the article appeared the Lord

spoke to Pearl Coleman and at last she heard Him and was obedient. Pearl wrote her updated testimony very soon after the events described. This was just as I was completing this book. A copy of the testimony was passed to me by Pearl, and I have included extracts from it.

Testimony of a Practitioner

"Because I was introduced to homoeopathy as a result of having been cured of a long-standing bladder/kidney problem by three homoeopathic pillules, I could not believe that it was satanic. I was plagued by cystitis, pyelitis and nephritis over a period of some seventeen years. Countless pyelograms, bladder washouts, antibiotics, hospitalisations and investigations under orthodox medical supervision proved useless.

Likewise, I had a history of sore throats with gaping ulcers that needed cauterisation with silver nitrate, and two tonsillectomies did nothing to help. Homoeopathy could abort these terrible throats overnight, whereas previously they had led to fever and pain and disability.

Lastly, I have endured a tendency to bleed prolifically after surgery. In particular I recall a nineteen week haemorrhage following anal surgery and bacteraemia which totally debilitated me and left an horrific blood picture. Homoeopathic medicine aborted the bleeding when I was virtually at the point of death. It was as serious as that! Never have I been so desperately ill.

Similarly at my Christian Clinic for Environmental Medicine, where I specialise in Clinical Ecology, (allergy tracing) diet, nutrition and prayer, I have used homoeopathy alongside natural herbs and vitamin and mineral therapy, with not a little success. There was an outstanding case of a lady of seventy-one who was saved amputation of a finger by using homoeopathy where nine months of orthodox treatment had failed. So how could it be occult?

In the October 1985 edition of "Christian Woman" I strongly defended the battalions of homoeopathy against

Andrew Macaulay of Reachout, a Christian ministry to people in the cults. This article I now retract, although my castigation of the sorcery of some orthodox medicine remains unchanged.

I was first prodded by a Holy Spirit arrow at a conference in 1985. But I deflected it with my intellect! I realise, of course, that it is true that the Lord gradually unfolds things that he wants us to stop, one step at a time, as we grow spiritually. I must say that six months ago I had a real stirring to perceive if I was in any way disobedient to him, and I started to examine myself daily, which is a matter of some discipline. I found it very strengthening to do this. Somewhere along the line there was always a check in my spirit and I could not quite put my finger on it. I had many Christians on one side being totally for homoeopathy and many Christians on the other side being against, and both sides contained members of the professions as well as sisters and brothers in my fellowship whom I greatly esteemed and respected in so many areas.

A few weeks ago the Clinic staff, every single member, went up on to the hillside to pray for Great Britain. It was absolutely bucketing down with rain and we had to seek shelter in a little country church. Before we started to pray for Britain I said to the girls, ''I want to get in agreement on prayer for a supernatural revelation on homoeopathy that is so clear I am not left in any doubt,'' and I said to the Lord, ''You know that as I have relinquished so much that is dear to me, I will relinquish this for you if you ask me to.'' We got into agreement and prayed, and as we prayed I was reminded of an incident when I had an extension in my roof space built earlier this year to use for increasing materials and equipment for the Clinic. I had decided that it would be a good idea to move the homoeopathic pharmacy upstairs and I spoke to the carpenter about designing me a special board to slot the bottles into the walls on a much wider scale than the pharmacy down below. Over the years I had collected £2,500 of homoeopathic medicines and many of the bottles had never actually been unstoppered, but a competent pharmacist always has to have the remedy to hand just in case it is needed for somebody. There were thousands of these bottles in three sizes.

It was quite an extraordinary thing to me when the carpenter concerned, a Christian gentleman, did not seem to come up with the goods. Upon questioning him he told me, ''I just cannot seem to drill the round holes the size you want in the wood without it splitting. I have tried all sorts of drills and there must be another tool but I cannot purchase one anywhere.'' I thought this was ridiculous, because the homoeopathic pharmacy downstairs had been created without any problem at all and holes drilled of all different sizes to hold the different sized bottles, by one who was not even a carpenter! So what was this man thinking of, and why could he not sort out the problem? When I prayed on the night that he told me this, I got a check in my spirit then and I chose to ignore it. It was a Holy Spirit arrow of truth.

All this was brought back to me in the church as I prayed with the staff. I knew the Lord was using me, but I also knew that I had to come to a time in my life when I had to be as perfect as I could be to be used by him, and this meant walking in complete forgiveness in all areas and being deceived by nothing and no one.

Following our prayer in the church, quite astonishing things happened. I had three patients say to me that they were much worse after taking homoeopathic medicines. This was my first experience of anybody doing this. One thing I had always been taught (and I studied under the Queen's homoeopathic physician) was that the blessing of homoeopathy was that if it did not do any good it never harmed you, but I had heard of two isolated cases where people claimed to have been harmed by homoeopathic medicines. I know that we were told that we could get a proving of a medicine which would mean that we were on to the right remedy but maybe the wrong potency, and as hard as I tried to convince myself that this was the case at the time these patients reported their distress, I had such a check in my spirit that I knew something was up. When this happened to the third patient, a very stiff upper-lipped, middle-aged lady of some fortitude and strength, but in very great pain with rheumatoid arthritis and with a very nasty skin problem of many years' duration, she broke down and wept in my consulting room because she felt so dreadful.

After she had gone, before I saw the next patient I asked the girls to come with me into the sitting room and pray a prayer that whatever revelation was to follow from the Holy Spirit I would not shrink from obedience, whatever it cost me. They, of course, just had to guess what was going on in my mind, but they both prayed earnestly for me.

As I continued to work that day I said to the girls, "Shut the homoeopathic pharmacy. I am not dispensing any medicines until hear from the Lord." In my heart I knew that those pharmacy doors would never open to dispense homoeopathy again.

The next morning I had to rise very early to go to Bible School. I asked my pastor to pray with me after the Bible School. I told him I had a feeling that I was going to abandon homoeopathy. I also told him I did not believe that it was occult. He said that he just felt peace when we prayed. I got home and went and looked at my homoeopathic library of very expensive books (one of them almost a collector's item), about £400 of books in all. I took them from the consulting room and oh! it did look bare. I chucked them into a dustbin sack and carted them downstairs. I started looking through the post and there it was, the coup de grace, a letter from an Anglican priest. He has a tremendous knowledge of demonology and has always helped me if I needed him at the Clinic. Twice I had prodded him about homoeopathy and he had not answered, and so again I had written him a letter and pressed him for a reply. (His reply included the following:)

"From my experience, those who use this form of medicine end up with a loss of Christian assurance. To lose one's grasp on such a fundamental thing as one's salvation is a very serious pastoral problem, and as a pastor I see it as a sinister attack on Christian life. I have known a number of people who have lost their peace and Christian assurance just before they died, so it seems to me that just when they needed the gift of assurance, they did not have it because they have been using homoeopathy. For non-Christians, they have no salvation and therefore a real peace of mind is neither here nor there for them on their deathbed.

If you really want to be used by God in this ministry of healing, may I *plead* with you that you have nothing whatsoever to do in the slightest way with occultism. Yours very sincerely, Jimmie.''

I rang him and an appointment was made. By that time I had started to empty my homoeopathic pharmacy. I realised that it was no good just smashing the bottles, but the contents had to be burned, as did the books, so I emptied out what I could and decided that I would salvage the bottles. As I was doing this I realised that I was reducing my income by half. I tipped out the granules and the powders into plastic bags, and I suppose I had already emptied about two hundred bottles when it was time for me to leave. I looked at the vast amount yet to be done and my heart sank. It was such a tedious job, with over one thousand medicines to go. I went to see Jimmie.

It is no use denying that since thousands of people use me as a GP I will not be able to mail out medicines or do repeat prescriptions for past patients who have always felt that a particular remedy suited them. However, I have unpacked the luggage that I have been carrying around with me since 1977. It took me fifteen laborious hours and my staff also spent time on it later.

I left him (Jimmie) and I looked at my beautifully bound leather books on the floor of his office. It was no problem for me to leave it all behind, none, because I have learned through tremendous pain that the only place to be is in the centre of God's will for peace, and the most dangerous place to be is outside his will.

Jimmie promised me that when one relinquishes something for the Lord He then reveals the next step, and I have known that the Clinic was changing in any event. I know, too, that my desire is to be involved in this work whilst not losing sight of the gifts that the Lord has given in being able to minister, and all he has taught me.

As a medical journalist I had written up the history of garlic so many times, and I know that it is one of the most useful and blessed of the herbs of the field that the Lord has given us for the service of man. The amazing thing is, it suddenly came to me like a mighty clap of thunder, I have not been prescribing it for a long time because unfortunately I used to say, "Garlic antidotes homoeopathic medicine." This is true, and homoeopaths will tell you so. Thus a counterfeit has been blocking healing with a natural herb! Garlic has been used successfully to treat leprosy, the plague, candidosis. It is antiseptic, and where used on patients' wounds in two world wars no gangrene developed. In fact our government advertised for people to grow it for one shilling a pound. What a revelation!

Since the homoeopathic pharmacy was burned, every sickness I ever cured with it has returned. Laryngitis, pyelitis, nephritis, ugly throats, fevers, everlasting coughs. As I write this, supported by the prayers of my fellowship, of friends and others, I continue to do battle. My finances have taken a shocking plummet and some formerly steadfast Christians have attacked me in an unprecedented manner. I am comfortingly assured, not least by the writer of this book, that this is the norm!! The author asks me how many Christians are turning to homoeopathy from orthodox medicine? It is difficult to give a figure — probably seventy-five per cent. Certainly Christians are homing in on homoeopathy, regarding it as a safe area of treatment in the hornets' nest of alternative medicine. They are alas deceived.

My own Clinic title, *Christian Clinic For Alternative Medicine,* was changed to *Christian Clinic For Environmental Medicine,* to avoid confusion that we were dabbling in the occult. Homoeopathy has had that taint only for the enlightened, of which I am now one. Praise God!''

Every testimony is personal and the Lord will continue to speak to Pearl as He will keep speaking to each one of us. The Lord can use books and testimonies but we each have to get our own revelation for ourselves.

I believe the hour is very late and that the Lord is calling forth watchmen who will blow the trumpet — not our own trumpet but the Lord's. In this way souls can be pulled back from the hands of the deceiver; bondages that take the lost further from the light and reduce the effective witness of Christians can be removed.

Part Three

Vehicles for the New Age in the Church : Their Destinations

10

Rome's Infiltration of the Charismatic Movement

I am happy to say that the fellowship of which I was a member was not involved in any unequal yoke with the Roman Catholic Church, and this is in spite of my own misdirected efforts as a young Christian to encourage this. Filled with a special brand of enthusiasm often seen in young Christians, in the first months as a born again believer I couldn't get enough of the things of God. Whilst I was active in our own quite large fellowship, there remained for me a free night, and unlike any other member of our fellowship I spent each Monday at a Charismatic Prayer Group. As far as I could see this just *happened* to be held in a Roman Catholic Convent School, and it just *happened* to be under Roman Catholic leadership. Things don't just *happen!* But as far as I was then concerned there also just *happened* to be a statue of the Madonna and Child standing in the corner of the room. I was, as I believed, totally teachable and totally for the Lord receiving more and more of Him from wherever I could get it! At the charismatic prayer group we had some outstanding visiting speakers, often with well-known names. There was good fellowship and the weekly gatherings were thoroughly enjoyable times.

The idol in the corner of the room was a constant reminder that things were not quite right, but what I did not know was that this sort of prayer group with Roman Catholic involvement, meeting regularly for worship and teaching, was what had been called the basic building block of the Charismatic

Movement. It was not for some months that I heard the Lord clearly. I had no problems with the fellowship but I had no option but to come out. I received the Word written in Colossians:

Beware lest any man spoil you through philosophy and vain deceit, after the tradition of men, after the rudiments of the world, and not after Christ. (Colossians 2:8)

Let the word of Christ dwell in you richly in all wisdom; teaching and admonishing one another in psalms and hymns and spiritual songs, singing with grace in your hearts to the Lord. (Colossians 3:16)

The Church of Rome and its faults *seemed* to be well understood by its charismatic members even though they could hardly be expected to view their church as a counterfeit. Such discernment comes when the involvement is renounced and the veil lifted. The charismatic Roman Catholic members could hardly be expected to see themselves as part of the whore of Revelation 17, but neither did I see that truth whilst I remained in that group. The Roman Church and its Pope who visited England at that time were much loved by all those I met among the Roman Catholic charismatics. I shared the two scriptures from Colossians (quoted above) with the leadership at the time I left the group, but beyond that it didn't seem my place to *admonish*. The Lord didn't seem to be wanting to use *me* to change things! Fellowship with Rome in this way seemed as natural and harmless as anything that could be imagined as far as the group was concerned. The Madonna and Child standing in the corner seemed quite natural too. It was there when my wife was a boarder at the School, there when she taught at the School, and it was there when our own daughter attended the school, but it came to be seen in a different light as a discerning Christian. The idol needed to be removed. It was with a sense of regret and some sense of failure that I left. I was still to get the revelation from Scripture which says:

Wherefore come out from among them, and be ye separate, saith the Lord, and touch not the unclean thing: and I will receive you. (2 Corinthians 6:17).

However in spite of what I didn't know, I was "out". The understanding came later. I was still to learn that these interdenominational prayer groups with Roman Catholic involvement and leadership stretched the length and breadth of the land and were focal points for many from the Roman Catholic, Anglican and "Free" churches who came into the charismatic experience. In these groups all can praise the Lord and be free to use the gifts together without the limitations of a pastoral authority and very often of a leadership having proper understanding of the breadth of Scripture. The result can be a focus on experience; the *"alive"* from among the *"dead"* non-Roman Catholic congregations come together with Roman Catholic people, and often Roman Catholic leadership. As we see from our brief look in this chapter* there is nothing *dead* about the Church of Rome. It is both an organism and an efficient organisation. It is very much *alive*.

The Strategy of Rome is Ecumenism

I believed it right to look at the origins (or roots) of the Charismatic Movement to see where the Roman Catholic connection came in. The Roman Catholic church had embarked on its strategy of ecumenism with Pope John XXIII and Vatican II. Vatican II was a worldwide ecumenical council of Roman Catholic bishops. "New Covenant" magazine serves the Roman Catholic church as an instrument of its renewal, and twenty-five years after Vatican II there appeared an article in January 1987 by its editor. The title was "Revelation; God reveals eternal truth to human beings through written and spoken words". The headline message was clear: "Vatican II documents teach that both Scripture and Tradition must be accepted and honoured with equal feelings of devotion and reverence" (capital letter for "Tradition" in the original). The Roman Catholic church *never* changes. It is only the strategy which changes.

---

* and more fully in "Understanding the New Age — Preparations for Antichrist's One World Government" by Roy Livesey (New Wine Press — 1986)

It is the counterfeit of the true Church and is described in Revelation 17. Accordingly its interest in the Charismatic Movement, and the fact that Pope John's initiative post-dated the start of the renewal in the Episcopalian and Anglican churches involving men like Dennis Bennett made Rome a subject for my attention. Having left the Charistmatic Prayer Group and renounced my involvement with it, I believe God was able to make some progress with me.

It was not of course a surprise that members of the Roman Catholic church were being saved. The surprise was that the Roman Catholics didn't come out of their counterfeit church when they *were* saved. I reasoned that I had come out of the occult world when I was saved, so why didn't they? It was a good question, and still is.

However, what now aroused my interest was the fact that the non-charismatic hierarchy and authority in the Church of Rome apparently were active in encouraging the Charismatic Movement and those of its members who participated in it.

Whatever the attitude at the level of the local priest, it is clear that the "seal of approval" is given from Rome. When I learned that Rome was interested in supporting the Charismatic Movement I regarded the matter as one for some caution. One leader of the Charismatic Movement reported that there are fifty million Roman Catholic charismatics in the world. The numbers include priests and nuns, bishops and at least one cardinal. The No.1 charismatic cardinal is Cardinal Leo Suenens of Malines-Brussels, Belgium.

Cardinal Suenens served the last two popes as liaison between themselves and the nine-man International Communication Office which served the Catholic Charismatic Renewal. Speaking at a Catholic Charismatic Conference in America, Suenens said the secret of achieving unity with the Holy Spirit in the best way was their unity with Mary the Mother of God. For this statement he got a standing ovation! One Evangelical reporting the conference for a leading Christian magazine left out this statement and gave a glowing picture of the so-called Evangelical Spirit of the Conference.

"If an Evangelical attends their meetings, he is thrilled by the spontaneous worship, the use of Scripture and also evangelical phraseology, but they seem to forget that most of the Roman Catholics are doing and saying things from a Roman context and background."*

On the Christian side David du Plessis was a significant leading figure and his burden for a unity including the Roman Catholics seems to trace back to 1961 when he lived in a Pentecostal Mission Station in Africa. He saw that the Roman Catholic and Protestant Missions were "bitter enemies of one another".** In "A Man called Mr Pentecost" David du Plessis describes the purging of his bitterness in those days in a special mass he attended during the Vatican Council in 1964:

"I felt myself melting and breaking, actually weeping openly as the mass unfolded .... I was aware even at that moment that the purging of my bitterness and suspicion had been complete."***

The same book describes St. Peter's Basilica when twenty thousand charismatics gathered at the Vatican for the 1975 Congress on Charismatic Renewal:

"Pope Paul stepped to his throne .... during the celebration of the Eucharist, there was singing with the Spirit, gently, tenderly, reverently and absolutely fitting. It was indeed a Pentecostal service, with Pentecostal manifestations and very evident Pentecostal blessings. All of us had prayed for a Pentecostal miracle to take place, but no one had expected such rich and positive manifestations of a new Pentecost ...."***

An influential Englishman, who has done a great deal of work to bring about the unity with Rome commented on the 1975 gathering in Rome of "Catholic Pentecostals"; he was encouraged by the Pope's endorsement of the Charismatic Renewal:

".... the Pope's endorsement of it is of great significance

* "The Charismatic Challenge" Seamus Milligan (E.P.S. Belfast)
** Logos Journal (Jan/Feb 1981)
*** "A Man called Mr Pentecost" by David du Plessis (Logos — USA)

155

and should be seen as an encouragement to all who are looking to the Holy Spirit to bring renewal to all the Churches."*

Another personality, well-known and influential, in the forefront of the launch of Roman Catholic pentecostalism, is Kevin Ranaghan. "Kevin Ranaghan can be credited with the tremendous advancement of Pentecostal Catholicism inside and outside the Church of Rome."* Ranaghan's writing makes clear the Roman Catholic definition of the church:

".... We believe that the Church of Christ subsists in the Catholic Church and that she possesses in unique fulness both revelation and the means of salvation. We are devoted to scripture, the teaching of the Church, the liturgy and sacraments, and the wisdoms of our spiritual tradition. We recognise that without our continual nourishment as sons and daughters of the Church throughout her many channels of grace, we will surely wither away. We place our own personal Charismatic experience in this context, and in the company of Mary and the Saints. With them as guides and models, we hope to stand as a beacon of truth and love in the midst of late 20th century fog and confusion. This is the scope of our life of faith. To say it encompasses less would be ecumenically and theologically dishonest."**

In 1969 Kevin and Dorothy Ranaghan told the "full story of the pentecostal movement in the Catholic Church — how it began, how it has spread ..."*** We read of greater devotion to Mary and to Roman Catholicism generally following the pentecostal experience. A reading of the 1983 edition **** shows the Renewal has come a long way. The International Catholic Charismatic Renewal Office is now an

* Quoted in "The Charismatic Challenge"
** From "The Church, the Spirit, and the Charismatic Renewal." Originally published in "New Covenant" Magazine (August 1981), P.O. Box 400, Steubenville, OH43952, USA.
*** "Catholic Pentecostals" (Paulist Press Deus Books — New York)
**** "Catholic Pentecostals Today" (Charismatic Renewal Services, South Bend, Indiana).

international ministry. Cardinal Suenens became involved in Renewal in 1973 and the office was run from Brussels. In 1981, the office moved to Rome, according to the Ranaghans, to be in better contact with the Holy See and with the many charismatic and other Church leaders who regularly pass that way.

Where have we got to in 1987? The Roman strategy is a worldwide one. The main thrust of a message given at an ecumenical gathering of several thousand charismatics from all over Europe at the N.E.C. Arena in Birmingham (the same 1986 gathering referred to in chapter eight) was to confirm and continue the march Romeward. We were told:

"Last January the Pope made a very important statement. He said that Europe needed to be re-evangelised. That wasn't anything new. But he said: and this task must be undertaken by all Christians united together in Europe. Tom Forrest* is a friend of the Pope and I wonder if we could ask him to take a message to the Pope from this conference: We're ready. We will join with you."

Let us not doubt that such statements from the popes *are* important. Let us not believe either that the plan for Europe is one quite apart from a global plan.

Vinson Synan is a leader in the Pentecostal-Holiness Church and a participant in the Catholic-Pentecostal ecumenical dialogues. He was one of the planners of a large ecumenical charismatic convention in Kansas City in 1977. Speaking of today's congresses held ten years after Kansas City, the North American Leaders' Congress on the Holy Spirit and World Evangelisation and the follow-up General Congress to be held in 1987, Synan expressed the belief that the Lord was telling all of them in the renewal that it's time to move in the power of the Spirit to evangelise the world. Speaking to the Roman Catholic "New Covenant" magazine, Synan, well-respected among Roman Catholic renewal leaders, said he believed "the next Billy Graham" may well be a Catholic. Rome is in the driving seat. She is taking the

---

* Tom Forrest is a leading member of the Roman Catholic Charismatic Renewal and was a main speaker at the conference.

initiatives. The infiltration is far gone, but even in 1971, referring to over forty thousand American Roman Catholics closely involved in the Catholic Pentecostal movement, we are told that the Roman Catholics were "truly on the march", "out-doing, out-witting and out-praying the Protestants."* Today Synan quotes a number of fifty million Roman Catholic charismatics in the world out of an estimated total of one hundred and fifty million. He sees a "*World* Congress on the Holy Spirit and World Evangelisation" in 1990. There plans will be presented for making the last decade of this century an extraordinary time of evangelism. "Our overall vision," Vinson Synan tells us "was given by Father Tom Forrest." It is to present to Jesus Christ over one half of the population of the world for His 2000th birthday.**

At the time of writing this section I received a poster for the "Walsingham Pilgrimage/Conference" to be held in August 1987. Walsingham is an English shrine, less well known than Lourdes and Fatima, but which attracts an increasing following of Roman Catholics, Anglicans and other visitors in these days. The theme of the conference is to be "New Dawn in the Church"; we are invited to send for details to "Our Lady Queen of Peace" at an address in London. Among the Roman Catholic priests, Jesuits and religious, was at least one distinguished speaker, the one with the now-familiar name, the man with the vision — Tom Forrest.

As mentioned previously, the message for Tom Forrest to take to the Pope from the Birmingham Arena was, "We're ready. We will join with you." The other message from Birmingham was "power evangelism". I believe there will be great emphasis during this so-called extraordinary time of evangelism upon what is becoming known as "power evangelism". Giving prominence to this as the means to "stir up" revival among Roman Catholic charismatics, Ken Metz, Chairman of the National Service Committee for the Catholic

* "None Can Guess" by Michael Harper (Hodder & Stoughton — 1971)
** See interview with Vinson Synan in "New Covenant" magazine (October 1986)

Charismatic Renewal in the United States, has written that "God is strengthening and stretching Catholic charismatics by showing us new ways to win souls for Jesus. His purpose is to enable us to evangelise the world during the last ten years of this century on a scale unheard of in history."*

We have already noted that Roman Catholics, using Scripture and evangelical phraseology, do so from a Roman Catholic background. For Roman Catholics the Church is *Rome*. Yet great numbers of non-Catholic charismatics have been led up the Roman road. They have come very close to Rome itself. They have searched for unity and reconciliation despite God's word in Revelation 18:4, and consequently they have been allowed to find what they seek. We can pick up the trail twenty five years ago to be reminded yet again that Rome never changes. The *strategy* changed in 1963. We now look at the work and life of John XXIII. Can we really follow his direction to a "new Pentecost"?

John XXIII — A New Pentecost?

Pope John XXIII was significant as Ignatius de Loyola was significant. Each marked a subtle change of tactic to win the Protestants to Rome. Loyola, already mentioned in chapter eight and referred to by the "Signs and Wonders" teacher as an example of one with a Christian healing ministry in the sixteenth century, was the founder of the Jesuits, who introduced occult "spiritual exercises", the new strategy to influence and gain control after the inquisition.

John's *purpose* was clearly stated in the "Documents of Vatican II" where he stated "The greatest concern of the Ecumenical Council is this: that the *sacred deposit* of Christian Doctrine should be guarded and taught more efficaciously ...." To his death it seems to me he believed, preserved and practised the same Roman Catholicism which was preserved intact. Out of it all came the ecumenical movement that we know today. In charge of it for Rome was the

* in "New Covenant" magazine (November 1986)

late Cardinal Bea who leaves us in no doubt about what is meant by the *"sacred deposit"* of the faith:

"No Catholic of education will believe that the council can or would change even a single dogma. The Supreme Pontiff and the council have a duty inherent in their ecclesiastical authority to preserve whole and entire the doctrine passed to them by tradition, and no love for the separated brethren can induce us to lay even the lightest hand on the *sacred deposit* of the faith." (my emphasis)*

In spite of the position of the Church of Rome the wave of ecumenism among professing Christians and of syncretism involving other faiths fast approaches us all. Rome has controlled kings and kingdoms. She is described in Revelation 17:4:

.... *the woman was arrayed in purple and scarlet colour, and decked with gold and precious stones and pearls, having a golden cup in her hand full of abominations and filthiness of her fornication.*

All down through history Bible teachers have identified the woman as the Church of Rome. Even the colours are right; purple and scarlet are the distinctive colours in the ecclesiastical robes of church dignatories. Millions were murdered by Rome during the Inquisition:

And upon her forehead was a name written, MYSTERY, BABYLON THE GREAT, THE MOTHER OF HARLOTS AND ABOMINATIONS OF THE EARTH. And I saw the woman drunken with the blood of the saints, and with the blood of the martyrs of Jesus: and when I saw her, I wondered with great admiration.   (Revelation 17:5—6)

The idols and images of Rome can be traced to Babylon. Another verse describes the seven hills on which Rome is built:

And here is the mind which hath wisdom. The seven heads are seven mountains, on which the woman sitteth"
(Revelation 17:9)

Certainly it can be expected that more groups will be

---

* Quoted from "The Identity of the Papacy" by Rev. J.A. Coleman (EPS — Belfast)

added back into Rome before the final scenario is complete.

Isn't it clear that Rome is the woman seated on the scarlet beast of Revelation 17? Certainly Luther, Wesley and the other great men of God from the past came to this conclusion. Solomon in Proverbs 7:27 warns against the adultress: *"Her house is the way to hell, going down to the chambers of death."* If so then born again Christians, believing they are acting in love and unity, are actually being deceived and used in the wider plan to establish a one-faith apostate Church. Jesus calls his people out, in order not to be defiled (Revelation 18:4). Remaining leads to defilement.

There is no value in *man*-made organisations, and whatever personal relationship Pope John may have had with Jesus, he was surely a significant figure in a new Roman Catholic strategy to unite what was lost in the Reformation and lead an ecumenical movement towards one-world religion with the Pope at the head. Unfortunately it will be the Apostate Church.

It needs to be emphasised that God loves Roman Catholics and *all* people. What we are considering in this chapter is the Roman "church" and the dangers of its doctrines to the real Church, the body of Christ. As we seek to contend for the faith (Jude 3) we need to discern Rome as the Lord sees it and so make a true assessment of the views of the many deceived believers. There will be an Apostate One-World Church and it is coming soon. The evidence and the Scriptures point conclusively to Rome, however bitter a pill that may be to swallow for those hoping for a change of heart and even doctrine. Rather than bringing about change Revelation 18:4 shows that they themselves will be defiled.

I have found that many profiles of Rome by those in the Charismatic Movement are generally unconvincing. One such profile is especially interesting. It is a book with the title of "Amazing John".

Amazing John!

"Amazing John" suggests that fresh air has blown through the Roman Catholic Church and that its spirit is changed. Its author, Fred Ladenius, once was in the Vatican Press Office serving the "church" in a variety of roles under Popes John XXIII and Paul VI. The following are the three concluding paragraphs of his book about John:

"Yes, prophets confirm the prophets, as the Scripture teaches us. Frank Buchman had spoken of a coming revolution, the last one, through which the cross of Christ would transform the world. Pius XII had proclaimed a new springtime. The vision of John XXIII had newly underlined the task that God gave to those He loves, which is to repair relationships, bringing truth, justice, love, and freedom into the world, bringing about peace through God-given order, as he said in his encyclical, "Pacem in Terris".

The extraordinary merit of Demos Shakarian (the Founder of the FGBMFI)* is to have been able to set up spiritual platforms where Christians, filled with the Spirit of Pentecost, meet together, freed by the bonds of a unity going beyond uniformity transforming the destiny of men and nations according to the plan of God. The FGBMFI is not a new church, but an arm of the church of Christ, men of every continent revealing to the world the power of the Resurrected One and the love of their Saviour, witnessing in season and out of season to what the Lord has done in their lives. You too can be involved today.

I know what I am talking about when I say that through the charismatic renewal, as through these men of the FGBMFI — men who have accepted everything God has to give, by His Holy Spirit, in order to be able to give in their turn — through these, the vision of a new Pentecost, as seen by John XXIII, is being made reality. It is a reality perhaps

* This refers to "Full Gospel Businessmens Fellowship International"

beyond our expectations, but certainly not beyond his."*

With those words the story of "Amazing John" was concluded.

As for Frank Buchman, the Founder of the cult of which I was once a member, he had a conversion experience after a Keswick Convention but ended up in a cult. Angelo Roncalli *started out* in the "church" of Rome, and there he remained in the biggest cult of all. He ended up as Pope John XXIII. God deals with each of us as individuals. Maybe he did finish up knowing Jesus. I hope so, but one evidently reliable report** based upon the hour-by-hour accounts recorded by the Vatican authorities, shows the dying Pope with the rosary entwined in his fingers, praying to the Virgin and saints, with his eyes fixed on their statues, and his confessor Mgr. Cavagna praying the prayer of the dying, also to the saints.

Pope John's "Journal"*** was a record in his own hand of a life from 1895, as a fourteen-year old, up to 1963, the year of his death. The first entry was: "First and main principle, choose a spiritual director …. on whom you may depend entirely …." The last entry was a prayer to Louis Palazzolo, a dead priest who had founded the Institute of the Sisters of the Poor:

"….O heavenly intercessor, obtain from God that the stream of holy fervour may be kept flowing among Christians …. that the fields ploughed for centuries may continue to bear their young and promising shoots ….

Through the grace of God may your example attract priests and religious, both men and women, scattered throughout the world …. (to) become the most enthusiastic co-operators in that hoped-for spiritual progress which the Church of this age, strengthened by the Ecumenican Council, wishes to

---

* "Amazing John" by Fred Ladenius. Copyright © FGBMFI Gramma, 1980. Used by Permission.
** "John XXIII" by Paul Dreyfus (Fayard — France)
*** "Pope John XXIII — Journal of a Soul" translated by Dorothy White (Geoffrey Chapman, a division of Cassell Publishers Ltd — London 1965)

achieve for the good of mankind."*

What more do we know of Louis Palazzolo? He had been beatified by Pope John on 19th March 1963. This means that Louis, because of the holiness of his life, deserves to be called "blessed" and is to be regarded as enjoying Heaven.** Or, as the Oxford Dictionary defines beatification, it is the announcement that the dead person "is in bliss".

Some of these Roman ways will seem far removed from the ways of many of the ecumenical Roman Catholics we meet in the movement Pope John re-established in the world. Yet we need to recognise these ways as occult ways. *"For there is one God, and one mediator between God and men, the man Christ Jesus"* (1 Timothy 2:5).

Whatever Pope John XXIII's merits may or may not have been as regards infiltration of the charismatic movement with Roman doctrinal error, what is certain is that there *has* been this infiltration. Roman Catholic charismatics, often eulogising John XXIII and encouraged by the Vatican of our own day, bring an added dimension to the deceptions found in the body of Christ and looked at in the previous chapters.

Rome and Authority

Rome would indeed not be Rome without Papal authority and the western world is moving fast in the direction of Rome. The so-called Christian Church seems to be throwing open all its doors in the name of ecumenism, or rather "unity". In the world's view the Catholic church is doing a great work around the globe and increasingly this seems to be the view of the body of believers. The following is extracted from a transcription of a taped interview with an Indian Roman Catholic nun, Sister Ann, who works in Katmandu, Nepal with Mother Teresa's organisation, Missionaries of Charity. All are doubtless sincere and we can only admire such self-sacrifice. Yet error has to be

---

* "Pope John XXIII — Journal of a Soul" translated by Dorothy White (Geoffrey Chapman, a division of Cassell Publishers Ltd — London 1985)
** "An Encyclopedia of Religion" (Philosophical Library New York — 1943)

exposed wherever the Lord leads, and not least for the sake of those who promote it. The date of the interview was 23rd November 1984:

INTERVIEWER: These people living here are dying and their bodies are being burned over at the river. What do you tell them to prepare them for death?

SISTER ANN: We are not allowed to teach anything about our religion, because we are strictly forbidden to talk religion (she is speaking of government restrictions). So we don't talk directly, but indirectly, according to their way. So they speak Bhagwan, no? (Hindu concept of a supreme being) So we tell them they are going to face the Bhagwan; prepare yourself. If you have hurt him in different ways or if you have offended him by your sin, try to make up with him. Say sorry to him. So they say, "Yes, we are sorry for what we have done." And they have their own confession in their own ways, you know.

INTERVIEWER: Their own gods and things?

SISTER ANN: Yes, so we also take the name of Bhagwan and tell them in that way.

INTERVIEWER: Do you believe if they die believing in Shiva or in Ram (Hindu gods) they will go to heaven?

SISTER ANN: Yes, that is their faith. My own faith will lead me to my God, no? So if they have believed in their god very strongly, if they have faith, surely they will be saved.*

Bible-believing Christians know that the only way to the Father is through Jesus. Satan purposes to deceive and show that salvation can be by other ways. He would have us focus on all the **evidence** the "good" people bring forth.

In the light of Bible truth we are able to weigh Mother Teresa's own doctrinal position. This is how she sees the authority of "Superiors", and is taken from "The Love of Christ"** where we see what "Mother Teresa speaks to her Religious — Delhi 20-9-1959":

---

* Reproduced from "Focus — Facts and Comment on the Current Religious Scene" (6 Orchard Road, Lewes, E.Sussex BN7 2HB, England — September 1985)
** Published by William Collins Sons & Co Ltd (Fount) — Glasgow 1982

".... Try to excel in obedience. Now that we have three local Superiors, help them by your cheerful and prompt, blind and simple obedience. You may be more talented, more capable, better in many ways, even more holy than your Superior. All these qualities are not required for you to obey. There is only one thing to remember, 'She takes the place of God for you.' "

Let us not be surprised; isn't it the Roman Catholic way? No Superior, no "Vicar of Christ" (one of the Pope's titles) nor anyone can stand between a true born-again believer and God. Only Jesus can be the Mediator; we are to keep our eyes on Him and on the *truth* of God's word.

In the next chapter we look at another group. In Shepherding/Discipleship there is a clear parallel to the ways of Rome. Yet in this movement we find a hotch-potch of belief and a hotch-potch of support. The focus, whilst unintentional, is on unity and experience rather than the Word. It even has leaders who, like Sister Ann, are universalists; "If they have believed their god .... surely they will be saved."

In Shepherding/Discipleship the usurping of the place of Jesus may be subtle at first. It may not even be the intention of the shepherd that his sheep submit to him, but in due time the position that Mother Teresa describes can be reached. Indeed the shepherd can "take the place of God for you."

11
Shepherding/Discipleship

In covering this Section it needs to be stated that we are looking at a Movement, not commenting on shepherding or discipleship as it may occur in any single fellowship. Rather it is the subtle control and restriction on believers which is a form of manipulation and as such biblically wrong. That it has become a Movement is more alarming than the odd case or situation.

I had read a great deal about the Shepherding/Discipleship movement in Britain and in the United States yet was hesitating about writing this chapter through lack of personal experience. Even the leaders, often drawn into it slowly, are mostly quite new to it. I found that those involved couldn't easily explain it. "It's not what you think" they would tell me. Then at length I was forced to consider the question: "Was I in a situation myself which was in truth a shepherding/discipleship situation?"

I was planning a visit to one of the Shepherding/Discipleship centres in the south of England. It had attracted a number of Christians whom I knew and who had what could be described as significant national and specialist ministries. In the event I believe the visit was unnecessary. An itinerant evangelist from that fellowship came to speak at a nearby crusade. It was possible to talk at some length with this man and his wife and I described our own situation. "That is Shepherding" he told me.

It is true that many in the Shepherding/Discipleship movement are not subject to what many in the movement defensively describe as "heavy" Shepherding; that was my own situation as I pondered if the heavy shepherding would come later. Of course shepherds (or pastors) *are* scriptural! However what Satan so often does is to *start* with Scripture. For him it's a sensible place to start; nor would he start with "heavy" shepherding. The danger manifests itself when the shepherd *starts* to take the place of Jesus. It needn't take long, nor is it always intentional.

In the previous chapter we have seen how papal authority and Roman Catholic dogma take the place of a personal relationship with Jesus. Though it may not be their own fault, and perhaps seldom would it be their wish, there are many shepherds who are reckoned to be above question in their teaching and decision making. What we are seeing here is a trend. Maybe the idea of Discipleship and Shepherding is no longer, in face of its critics and the changing views of its founders, quite so fashionable. Yet it is *ideas* that get a hold and a Shepherding/Discipleship *spirit* is at work. The battle is being fought in the spiritual realm (Ephesians 6:12). The leaders are scriptural in large part yet the shepherd who will not contend for the faith (Jude 3) is vulnerable; while he focuses on his covering and the submission of his flock to him, there are many doctrinal errors, vital but little understood by the movement's shepherds or sheep, that are creeping in.

Certainly it is difficult to generalise about such a changing movement which has such a mixture of doctrines — doctrines that can be tracked down (often taking some effort) in books and tapes, but which are not the required ingredient in the mixture for bringing the pastoral care and harmony between shepherd and sheep. The groups vary. There has been trial and error in this relatively new movement. Mistakes made in one group are reckoned when starting the next. However well intentioned though it all may be, their authority structures, the lack of any solid Bible base or even some good tradition, has naturally brought a focus on the doctrines of those shepherds at the top of the pyramid structure.

Individual personality differences and influence cannot of course be eliminated, and as shepherding has grown through the house church movement in Britain there has been the opportunity for personalities to emerge, particularly through the annual camp gatherings with opportunities to promote books and reach large audiences.

In the Shepherding/Discipleship environment the place of the Bible is reduced. One very colourful charismatic organiser of one of these camps has gone on the record in 1986 to declare that he doesn't believe in the inerrancy of Scripture. It's a doctrine that can't be proved, we are told, since all the original manuscripts are lost! The doctrine of Bible fallibility is at least consistent with that of papal or shepherd infallibility with the shepherd lording it over his flock! Paul didn't lord it over the Corinthians. He wrote to them: *"Not for that we have dominion over your faith, but are helpers of your joy: for by faith ye stand"* (2 Corinthians 1:24).

We take a closer look at the "kingdom" in chapter thirteen. Suffice to say here that the Shepherding/Discipleship movement in Britain has been a significant vehicle for this kingdom-building. It was at the same 1986 Festival that we were introduced to another gospel by another spirit through the person of a leading New Ager, not a Christian at all! It is one of the propositions of this book that the Kingdom people and the New Agers are perilously headed for the same mistaken goal. That is our subject for chapter fourteen.

The Idea Came From America

Shepherding/Discipleship is relatively new having started in the United States in the early 1970s. It was based upon the teaching of the Argentinian, Juan Carlos Ortiz, and we can now see the evidence of major errors well-launched into the body of believers through the Movement. We have been subtly led away from the Word of God. In "The Christian and Authority" it is put like this:

"His (the leader's) interpretation of Scripture and the will of God is held to be *automatically* superior to the ordinary believer by virtue of his 'anointing'. Often such leaders will not hesitate to pronounce God's will for the minutiae of their followers' personal lives.''*

It is *ideas* that are important — and the *spirit* that takes them over. Here was a new doctrine with some biblical justification that was attractive to Man. The foundation is obedience. Jesus required His disciples to obey Him without question! In Shepherding/Discipleship the rationale appears to be that if your shepherd tells you to do something and you know it to be wrong, God will honour you for your obedience to the shepherd. As a new Christian I believed that myself.

The movement seems to grow by a system of "covering". A fellowship gets linked into the system as its leader gets covered by another who is styled an apostle or who, in one way or another, is already in the system. Shepherding/ Discipleship teaches the doctrine that every believer needs a fellow-believer as a "covering". Like any movement it needs money. It grows by the "tithing" and the giving by its members. It grows by borrowing too. The spending budgets are large. Outreach projects, specialist activity like TV and expansion generally, inevitably make substantial finance necessary. In one case I was saddened to hear of members being encouraged to raise second mortgages on their homes to raise finance for group activity. Growth comes too through the opportunities presented to leaders and prospective leaders. Obviously it's attrctive to get the "right" men on the team. Colourful and charismatic men are good for bringing growth in numbers, and for them their security in the group can be a key to self-confidence and speaking opportunities that would otherwise be out of reach. There can be appearances at the big rallies and festivals where audiences number many thousands.

* Article by Elliot Miller in "Forward" — Spring 1985 (Christian Research Institute, San Juan Capistrano, California)

True Shepherding

Certainly God will use biblical shepherds, but under the New Covenant there is no need of 'anointed' men like Moses for the Bible tells us that God has put His laws in our hearts and on our minds (Hebrews 8:9). We have Jesus. *"For there is one God, and one mediator between God and men, the man Jesus Christ"* (1 Timothy 2:5). Good leadership will encourage us *"to come boldly unto the throne of grace, that we may obtain mercy, and find grace to help in time of need"* (Hebrews 4:16).

As with Roman Catholic and cult activity, Shepherding/ Discipleship leaders take the role of mediator away from Jesus. The true shepherd will base his teaching upon the Word of God, on *all* of it and not simply on the passages that suit. For our part as believers we recognise *God's* authority in the local church. Hebrews 13:17 gives clear authority to leaders and we *are* to submit to them. However it is a *conditional* authority, one we are free to question when it is in conflict with Scripture. "The Christian and Authority" also provides the balance as we consider the trends in Shepherding/Discipleship:

"There is no question that Scripture grants the New Testament leader authority in terms of directing church affairs (1 Timothy 3:5), teaching and maintaining sound doctrine (2 Timothy 3:1—4), correcting those who sin, and taking disciplinary action if they refuse to repent (Titus 3:10—11). The believer who clearly violates Scriptural standards of behaviour has no grounds upon which to claim that he is following Christ according to his conscience, for his conscience should be informed by the word of God. In such cases, *church* authority, exercised properly, will help (rather than hinder) the Christian to submit more fully to *Christ's* authority.

The keynote of Jesus and the apostles' teaching on New Testament leadership, however, is clear: the pastoral ministry is to be marked by a servant's attitude and exemplary character, not by an emphasis on authority and submission

171

(e.g. Matthew 20:25—28; 1 Peter 5:1—3; 2 Corinthians 1:24).''*

Thus it is clear that there is a right and biblical way of discipling and the truth of that is not to be minimised.

I believe the road on which many are embarking is one that takes followers away from some important Bible truths. The damage done cannot be measured apart from the effect on believers of taking their eyes even for one moment off Jesus and His Word. Roman Catholics lived for years without access to the Word of God and many in that faith still do not have a Bible today. The Reformers decided that the Bible was indeed reliable and, by the Holy Spirit, easy to understand. They decided that Scripture contained all that was needed for Christian faith and living. They agreed with Paul: *"All scripture is given by inspiration of God, and is profitable for doctrine, for reproof, for correction, for instruction in righteousness."* (2 Timothy 3:16—17).

Covenant Commitment

Whilst the issues of covering and submission are important ones, even more serious doctrinal error is found in the little-understood theology of what has been called Covenant Commitment and Covenant Discipleship. This is found in Shepherding/Discipleship groups and involves the distortion and misuse of the Lord's Supper. The Lord's Supper wasn't to 'bind the disciples together' and such teaching is wrong. Jesus made no acknowledgement at the Last Supper of any covenant other than to keep His suffering and death constantly before us.

However, and as one American writer confirms, getting to the heart of Covenant Commitment and Covenant Discipleship doctrine is difficult:

"Endless rhetoric, layer upon layer of complicated explanations and purposely vague ramblings, send the enquirer off on a mental goose-chase. This is typical of most

* "The Christian Authority" by Eliot Miller (article in "Forward" — Spring 1985, Christian Research Institute)

religions, "deep truth" movements, and of course cults such as the Covenant Discipleship Movement …. The problem in detecting cultism within the church is relatively new to evangelical Christianity …."*

Perhaps the most dangerous results of the trend in Shepherding/Discipleship are not with submission and shepherd's authority but with what we have in cults generally; Man is usurping Christ's position. Jesus wants to keep His death constantly before us. The communion reminds us that we owe both our salvation and our complete wholeness in Him to His grace. Relationships with one another in the body of Christ are very important, but the communion is about our relationship *with Jesus*. The new covenant is not a matter of acknowledging a commitment to one another, but *to Jesus*. Surely a man has to put things right with his brother, but the covenant is a covenant *with Jesus*. Of course the Corinthian church was unruly. They needed to understand the difference between an orgy of food and wine and the remembrance of Jesus with the new covenant in His blood (1 Corinthians 11:25). Paul warned them it was a covenant *with Jesus*.

It seems clear Jesus made no acknowledgement of establishing any covenant at the Last Supper other than the new covenant in His blood. The carnal gratification enjoyed by the Corinthians at the Lord's table was a joy to Satan. The shifting of the singular place of Jesus at His own table continues today.

Of course there can be no place for "nit picking" and we have to obey our leaders where we can. It is also true that we have to be subject to one another in fear of Christ (Ephesians 5:21). We are warned too against not meeting together, and all the more as we see the Day approaching (Hebrews 10:25). We have to get the balance right. No-one is saying that the Lord is not using the leaders in Shepherding/Discipleship. Indeed He can and will use anyone. Many are coming to a saving knowledge of Jesus Christ

* "False Cult Emerges from Charismatic Movement" (from Special Edition of "Daystar Herald" — Evangelical Press Association, USA)

173

through some of the people who make up the movement. What can be said to our brethren in this movement is: "Check it out with Scripture." In this way the balance will be corrected.

The Lord's Return?

Many in Shepherding/Discipleship, even among the leaders, have not reached the place of making the end-time scriptures a subject for serious study. The early return of Jesus is much mentioned from the pulpit and yet the scriptures relating to the end-time seem to arouse little interest. In the next chapter we take a look at another area which has exercised my own discernment, and once again it is an error that flows from Shepherding/Discipleship ideas. The spirit at work in Shepherding/Discipleship takes the focus off Jesus's personal return just as it takes attention from His physical body at the Lord's Supper. Instead of expecting Jesus to catch us up in the clouds to meet the Lord in the air, the teaching at work through the Shepherding/Discipleship movement takes hold of the idea of a return into the literal physical bodies of the believers. Many will find that to be incredible, and of course many involved in Shepherding/Discipleship will say, "I've never heard that." Indeed teachers do use different words as we shall see but this is what it amounts to and there is little argument over doctrine. These are the believers who are "building the Kingdom", and we shall see what that means to many in Shepherding/Discipleship when we understand what is meant by "Restoring the Kingdom". As I probed the writings on this subject I found there was more to it than submission, covering and commitment. Man was shifting the Lord off His own Table. But, more than that, Man was also stealing the Lord's return.

There will be a measure of "Shepherding/Discipleship" in many fellowships. No pastor or fellowship can be completely free of error for our walk with the Lord is one that always takes us *further* into truth. A pastor is properly the shepherd of his flock. He has a personal relationship with the Lord as we all do. He has a personal relationship with each member of his flock, and will be guided as the Lord leads in each relationship. There can be no rules or law in any given situation and what I have sought to do in looking at Shepherding/Discipleship is to sound the alarm against bringing an undue focus on a leader to the exclusion of the person of Jesus Christ. As Christians we need to learn our lesson by looking at the cults. If our relationship isn't first and foremost with Jesus then we have nothing of value.

It is no part of the purpose to bring condemnation on members of these groups, nor indeed upon the members of other Christian ministries described in the book. To test the prevailing teachings is not being negative. We have to do it because the Bible requires it. The best known example is Paul's reproof of Peter in his letter to the Galatians. He also says in that letter: *"But though we, or an angel from heaven, preach any other gospel unto you than that which we have preached unto you, let him be accursed."* (Galatians 1:8).

The Shepherding/Discipleship movement comprises born-again Christians who are focusing, imperceptibly at first, on themselves and their leadership. The seeds of the error can be discerned by those who have eyes to see. For others heeding seducing spirits and the doctrines of devils, which the Bible speaks about for the latter times, the bondage becomes greater, and the wrong path will only lead to further deception.

Many will say that the time of excesses in Shepherding/Discipleship is past, that the pyramid of control has been turned upside down. The evidence seems to be that little has changed. The Shepherding/Discipleship movement moves ahead quietly, without much fuss, and attracting little attention. In "Daystar Herald" we read, ".... the problem in detecting cultism within the Church is relatively new to evangelical Christianity. For some it is too shocking to believe, much less accept. Still, Jesus Himself prophesied that in the last days false prophets would arise and seduce many, even the elect if it were possible (Matthew 24:24)."

The Apostle Paul confirms this in his letter to Timothy:

> *Now the Spirit speaketh expressly, that in the latter times some shall depart from the faith, giving heed to seducing spirits, and doctrines of devils.* (1 Timothy 4:1)

"So how is one to know when such spirits are present in the Body of Christ? Having a good knowledge of the Word is helpful but not enough. What is needed, and sorely lacking in the Church today, is much sharper discernment of those who teach doctrine."*

> *Beloved, believe not every spirit, but try the spirits whether they are of God: because many false prophets are gone out into the world.* (1 John 4:1)

"With this discernment will come a healthy, fearless scepticism of any new revelation said to be coming from God. By blending knowledge, experience, and discernment with a godly jealousy for the truth, that which is false can be uprooted and forced out into the open .... We in the Church are used to thinking of cult activity only in terms of those teachings that are completely outside of the scriptures and that do not answer directly to the Bible — Virgin born, the Son of God and Saviour of the world. While this is still a good measure, cult activity needs to be redefined today to include any movement which, while continuing to identify itself with fundamental Christianity, in fact teaches contrary to it."*

Judging/Discerning other Believers and other Doctrines

Another contributor to "Daystar Herald" makes the point that the recent growth of Covenant Discipleship as a movement is due to the prevailing view among charismatics that we should never judge other believers; "the modern charismatics developed this liberal 'tolerance policy' as a means of bridging the traditional, doctrinal gap between the various denominations that individual charismatics continue

* "Daystar Herald"

176

to represent. But continually ignoring doctrinal differences in the name of 'love' can have disastrous repercussions. For although we are called upon to love one another despite our differences, we must not make the tragic mistake of placing sound doctrine so far down on our list of priorities that consequently we allow false doctrines to proliferate, false teachings like the Covenant Discipleship Movement to go on uncorrected, and an unscriptural 'I'm OK, You're OK' attitude to become habitual.''* In fact the Bible clearly teaches that it is given to the believer to *judge* or to *discern* all things. The same Greek word ''anakrino'' is translated to mean ''discern'' in 1 Corinthians 2:14 and to mean ''judgeth'' in 1 Corinthians 2:15:

> *But for the natural man receiveth not the things of the Spirit of God; for they are foolishness unto him: neither can he know them, because they are spiritually discerned.*   (verse 14)
>
> *But he that is spiritual judgeth all things, yet he himself is judged of no man.*   (verse 15)

''Obviously then, the ability to judge or discern between what is good and what is evil in all the various denominations, doctrines, and teachings that are gone out into the world is an essential, God-given gift. This is especially true today when, if it were possible, the very elect would be deceived.''*

The Church — Accountability to Each Other

As Christians we are immediately under God's authority through His Word. The Bible nowhere suggests we are independent of our fellow believers but the effect of a structure such as we see in the Shepherding Movement is to encourage members and shepherds to check things out with the man above rather than with one another. Paul urged the Ephesians to submit *''yourselves one to another*

* ''Daystar Herald''

177

in the fear of God'' (Ephesians 5:21). No Christian is an island and we should not stand on our own for God has so equipped us that we each have something valuable to contribute, and we each need what the others have to give. While in one sense the Bible teaches us to be accountable to each other, there is another sense in which we shall be completely accountable only to God. We shall be unable before God to blame the pastor or shepherd for the wrong teaching we have followed; the Holy Spirit must be our teacher. If the Bible clearly upholds a particular truth, then even when the entire church is moving in the opposite direction, our responsibility is to follow the will of God and not the wishes of the church we are attending. Let us not lose sight of the dilemma which faced Paul at Antioch where Peter, while in the liberty of the Gospel, had been eating with the Gentiles in spite of the variance from Jewish tradition. Then after men, who came from James (Galatians 2:12) came on the scene, Peter, fearing what they would think, "began to withdraw and set himself aloof."

Peter was a man of great stature like many of our charismatic pastors and shepherds of today; when he stood back, the other Jewish Christians who had been associating with the Gentiles also made themselves aloof. Even Barnabas who had been Paul's closest associate and who probably knew as well as most the issues that were at stake was also carried away with their hypocrisy (Galatians 2:13).

Paul soon found he was the only Jew left at the Gentile table and though he no doubt respected Peter, he saw the very essence of the Gospel was in danger of being altered through bringing in tradition that had no place in New Testament Scripture. Peter's authority in that situation was only conditional and when he chose to move away from the principles of the Gospel, he also moved away from its authority and the authority it gave him. This important event recorded in Galatians 2 presents a significant message to those involved in the Shepherding Movement and to those in fellowships who, even without realising it, may be moving in that direction. The Word of God has an authority totally distinct from the Church, and the Church holds no authority when it departs from it. Paul was already very positive in Galatians 1 where he wrote:

> *But though we, or an angel from heaven, preach any other gospel unto you than that which we have preached unto you, let him be accursed.* (Galatians 1:8)

No man can change the Gospel. Its authority is absolute.

12

The Manifestation of the Sons of God

There is one often-forgotten body of doctrines that was around long before the start of the present charismatic movement. Presented in different ways, through different groups and teachings, it is a movement that is alive but not much noticed and having the very descriptive title of the Manifest Sons of God. This doctrine was declared a heresy by the Assemblies of God in America in 1950; the Latter Rain movement in 1948 had provided the vehicle for the doctrines to get a far wider acceptance and clarification.

These doctrines revolve around some vital scriptural interpretations. Scriptures on the resurrection or redemption of the body are not taken to refer to the Lord's return when we are caught up to meet Him in the air at what Christians have called the Rapture; instead these scriptures are thought to be fulfilled by a select group of "overcomers", the "Sons of God", while here on earth. They believe they will be sinless and immortal in their physical bodies when they become manifest as the Sons of God. The scriptures referring to being caught up in the air to meet Jesus and be taken to the throne of God are thought to have their fulfillment at this manifestation of the Sons of God.

Manifest Sons of God — Christ Corporately and Individually

Manifest Sons believe they will become Christ both corporately and individually. They consider the corporate body of Christ to actually be Christ. That is the measure of the deception of those deeply rooted in the Manifest Sons philosophy; most of those drawn subtly into Manifest Sons teaching have not yet gone that far. Nevertheless, are not those who take their eyes off the Lord's death and put an overemphasis on the corporate body at the communion table well started along that deceptive road?

The corporate body of Christ is seen as Rome sees the Church, as a sort of external extension of the incarnation of Christ. They see scriptures referring to His ruling the nations and judging the world as finding fulfilment through themselves. They make a distinction between Christ's coming, appearing or manifestation to rule and judge the world through the Sons of God and His later individual, personal return. He is said to be unable to return personally until the stage is set by the establishment of His rule and reign through the Sons of God subduing the nations, taking DOMINION, and executing judgment on the ungodly. On the view of the Manifest Sons, when this is done we shall be into a new age. Perhaps they intend a different meaning of ''new age'' from the one used throughout this book, but I believe the choice of words is prophetic and that we may expect an eventual merge into the New Age movement. The Manifest Sons look to the new world order, the theocracy, divine government, a divine order, or — more familiarly — the *Kingdom Age*. The stage would then be set for what Manifest Sons would see as Jesus Christ's return. Yet would the scene be viewed any differently by the *New Age* people? Are not those who pick up Manifest Sons doctrine running the great risk of becoming so deceived that they will fail to discern the true identity of the false Christ when he appears?

I believe we can see a single thread running through the teaching of various apparently different Christian ministries — a thread that gives them a clear identity with the Manifest Sons of God message. While, for example, the challenge of the error in ''submission'' and ''covering'' and all the rest in say the Shepherding/Discipleship movement is vital and important, let us consider an issue perhaps even more far-reaching in its significance. Let us consider carefully the influence of the spirit that is at work to prepare the world for the false Christ through false teaching about the Rapture. Let us consider how those Christians unwilling to hear the watchmen could find themselves unknowingly misleading others into a unity with out-and-out New Age people coming up over another horizon.

"You're Looking at God; You're Looking at Jesus"

One summer I attended a one-week teaching conference in Birmingham. The teacher who appeared to us on a big screen was a very well known American evangelist. There were about a thousand of us there. It was powerful teaching that seemed to be very good, though there were a few strange things that I was prepared to overlook, things I just couldn't put my finger on.

Then last year I was sent some tapes of this evangelist's summer school in Toronto, Canada. I hadn't heard his message put quite like this before though I had learned already that the message of some Americans could be more "advanced" when delivered in America, and more exploratory and cautious when given here. The label on the plastic folder presented the tapes in an attractive way and I read of the "anointed message" on "The end-time Manifestation of the Sons of God". I listened to the first tape and heard the man I had seen on the big screen. What was at work inside us, he said, is that manifestation of the expression of all that God is and all that God has. He was telling his audience they weren't looking at him. "You're looking at God, You're looking at Jesus," he said.

Manifest Sons "Theology"

The Manifest Sons of God believe they will not only become

Christ corporately; they believe they will become Christ individually too. Jesus is reckoned to be the "Pattern Son", the first one to achieve the status as a divine, immortal, sinless Manifest Son of God. Today a growing movement can be discerned. *Discernment* and some understanding is necessary. Just as the New Age people "network", with one another and between groups, to form the New Age Movement, there is a similar loose linking of groups. The result is a Christian movement of great significance, which is like no other. The message is "the Kingdom Message"; biblical-sounding titles referring to themselves as "Overcomers" and of course "Manifest Sons of God" are among the clues to an involvement, knowingly or unknowingly, in the movement.

"Full Sonship", "Perfection", "Body Salvation" or the "Third Salvation" is reached (after the pattern) and at this point the glory of the Father is to inhabit the physical body. This "Christ Company" (now individually manifest as Sons of God) would then be revealed to the world as Many Saviours who would take dominion (establish theocracy or God's Rule) and execute judgement (annihilation of the ungodly). This is sometimes called the Great and Terrible Day of the Lord (Joel 2:31, Malachi 4:5) — great for those who receive the Manifest Sons of God and therefore alive to inherit the Kingdom, terrible for those who reject and are therefore taken in death and judgement. The present economic, religious and political systems are identified as Babylon and they will see their downfall through this *Great and Terrible Day* in which the Sons of God are Manifest.

That is the way the "theology" runs according to one account from America. Strange it may be to many, even maybe to those who are close to the teaching but blinded to an understanding, it is as well to have set down the outline at this early point in the chapter.

A quotation by Richard Baxter (1615—1681), a great man of God who lived in Kidderminster the town of my birth, caught my attention. Just one sentence sums up the danger of the road upon which the Manifest Sons of God seem to be embarked: "The most dangerous mistake of our soul is, to take the creature for God, and earth for heaven.''*

The Latter Rain Movement

The Latter Rain Movement, which gave a boost to Manifest Sons of God doctrine, began in Canada in 1948 and spread to the USA. It was thought of as the last great spiritual outpouring to consummate God's plans and see the return of Christ. The necessary perfection of the Church was expected to come about through submitting to the restored ministry of apostles and prophets, men who would be restoring truths lost to the Church and receiving new revelations. One Christian research organisation in California reports that there can be seen many kinds and types of teaching that can be traced back to that initial Latter Rain Movement. It points to present day schools of thought such as 'Positive Confession', 'Restoration', 'Shepherding', 'The Kingdom Message' and the 'Manifest Sons of God'. This movement also touched the Identity groups (Anglo-Israelism), 'Sacred Name Movement', and the 'Jesus Only' or 'Oneness' churches, giving to some of them extra doctrines. It adds that the history and present theology of the Manifest Sons of God groups is intertwined with all of these other movements which each profess one or more of their differing tenets. We have met these teachings in earlier chapters.

In advance of looking at the Restoration Movement in the next chapter, it can be made clear now that many leaders in the movement would not feel any identity at all with the Manifest Sons of God even given some better understanding of the heresy. In many cases that would be quite reasonable for *Restoration* describes a broad *movement* not a denomination. It includes many who are growing in their Christian walk through teaching that majors on faith and on the promises of God and who have benefited, as I have, from dynamic vibrant fellowships preaching the Word with signs following. *Manifest Sons of God* on the other hand, in

* "The Saints Everlasting Rest" by Richard Baxter

England at least, is relevant for its identification as a *doctrine* and as one that is difficult to clearly define. It is a warning to be on the look out!

When looking on the one hand at a subtle and not-very-clear doctrine, ideas, in groups not majoring at all on doctrine, and on the other hand at a very broad range of such groups, it would be very unfair to make any sort of blanket connection between Restoration groups and the excesses of Manifest Sons doctrine identified in America and briefly described in this book. Rather it is for each one of us to get a grasp of Scripture, and discernment, as it applies to the situations in our own fellowships and Christian groups. This is so whatever umbrella word describes the group, but it helps to have some awareness of the heresies that have particular relevance in individual situations.

Thus it is not my purpose to do more than point to the particular vulnerability of groups, like Restoration churches, when little understood heresies get even a toe-hold of acceptability. Furthermore it is recognised as far as Manifest Sons of God and Restoration are concerned, that a greater distance will separate them in the less advanced British situation. Yet once again we are well reminded that ideas are powerful and it is these which cross the world at speed. We are much helped in our understanding by looking at the North American experience.

William Branham

In the beginning of the Latter Rain Movement in North America, one of the men involved in the Sharon Orphanage, where the movement began, wrote an article entitled "How This Revival Began".* In it he attributed *two* main influences for the revival. One was William Branham and his healing ministry.

William Branham had been dead for many years and I had never heard the name until one day I met with a Christian

---

* By Ernest Hawtin in "The Sharon Star" (1st August 1949)

brother who introduced me with enthusiasm to Branham's extraordinary beliefs. He described Branham's "Serpent Seed" revelation to me. Eve is said to have had intercourse with the serpent, and the result was Cain. Of all Branham's beliefs this was perhaps the most extraordinary. I believe God had got my attention!

So who was William Branham, and what did be believe? Helped by Branham's original writings, it did not take long to put together a picture of the man and his ministry. His religious views included a mixture of various occult ideas. I later found out that many accepted Branham went wrong in the end of his life but for my part I was left wondering if Branham's ministry was *ever* soundly based. Gordon Lindsay in "William Branham — a man sent from God"* quotes Branham's own words as he described the voice that spoke to him when he was seven years old. "Never drink, smoke, or defile your body in any way, for I have a work for you to do when you get older." In Branham's words, this frightened him. He cried, ran home and never told anyone about it. Describing his childhood he said there was always that peculiar feeling, like someone standing near him, trying to say something to him, and especially when we has alone. No-one seemed to understand him, he thought. In describing his adult life, Branham tells of the words spoken to him by one sent from the presence of Almighty God: If you will be sincere and can get the people to believe you, nothing shall stand before your prayer, not even cancer.

The angelic visitation was in 1946 and the story of William Branham has been described as so out of this world and beyond the ordinary that were there not available a host of infallible proofs which document and attest its authenticity, one might well be excused from considering it far fetched and incredible. Indeed it seems his ministry *was* the most powerful and dramatic of all the healing revivalists. However, whilst documents and testimony can authenticate power, it is *discernment* we need in order to know from

* Published by William Branham (Jeffersonville, Indiana — 1950)

which source the power comes. By the late 1950s Branham's ministry had declined substantially. He died on Christmas Eve 1965 after a head-on collision with a drunken driver. He was buried on Easter Sunday, April 11th, 1966 and it is said this was due to his followers' belief that he was going to rise from the dead.

The following year, in 1967, William Branham's son quoted Malachi 4:5 in the introduction to five hundred and seventy-nine pages of Branham's writings*: *"Behold, I will send you Elijah the prophet before the coming of the great and dreadful day of the Lord."* He believed The Word of the Lord had promised that He would send to the earth once again the spirit of Elijah in the form of that End Time Messenger who was the angel to the Seventh Church Age in these final closing days of time. It was believed firmly that this promise was fulfilled in the vindicated ministry of William Branham.

I do not write as one who cares to rush to explanations, but surely the Branham story is a cautionary one for those who will listen to the Manifested Sons of God and the big names in our own day. Dr. Andrew Walker, in "Restoring the Kingdom" writes of his visit to a Branham meeting: "I remember as a boy listening to Branham's raucous Southern voice and hearing his amazing diagnostic talents when he claimed that he could see colours (or auras) that helped him correctly diagnose illnesses."** Certainly God can use any way he chooses, and I wasn't there, but one is in some difficulty finding such an example in Scripture. Yet, in the occult realm, many are seeing these auras today. As a "searcher" in that realm I met folk who saw auras in that way. From my reading I discovered that not only did Branham reject the orthodox belief in the trinity of the Godhead, but he also mingled in ideas about the Zodiac and the Great Pyramid. Not surprisingly, some of his ideas about Jesus were equally bizarre. I found this quotation of Branham's: "As I've often made this remark, and said, God

---

* "The Revelation of the Seven Seals" (Spoken Word — Tuscon, AZ)
** "Restoring the Kingdom"(Hodder & Stoughton, 1985)

made three Bibles. The first one, He put It in the sky, the zodiac .... He made the next one in the pyramid, back in the days of Enoch, when they made the pyramid." Branham's healing ministry was foretold by the visitation of a supernatural being who supposedly told Branham, "I would be able to detect diseases by vibrations on my hand." This is one of the methods used by healers involved in the occult.

Before we move on and consider the jigsaw pieces connecting William Branham, the Manifest Sons of God, the Latter Rain and those groups already looked at who combine together in the building of the Kingdom, let us once again stress that the need is for *discernment*. We look not to our own understanding, but in all our ways we seek to follow Him who will make straight our paths (Proverbs 3:5). We can only know these ways as we stay close to Him. It is a mystery but the Bible makes full provision for us to hear Him and be obedient. Satan's ways are a mystery too. The Bible calls them the "mystery of iniquity". Many writers, perhaps most, including some of the valuable authors I have quoted, whilst giving many clues to ministries like Branham's, do not distinguish the two realms of the supernatural. As Christians we need to know what is of God. I relate a personal story in this connection:

"George and the Dragon" — A Personal Word from the Lord

During the visit to the United States described in chapter one I was given an essay on the Manifest Sons of God that was at that time beyond my understanding. I had never before heard of the movement known as the Manifest Sons of God.

This unpublished essay (which we look at later in this chapter) was in many ways the most extraordinary document that ever came into my hands. It connected well-known Christian "names" in the United States with the Manifest Sons of God. I felt strongly that this would have a very significant place in my writing about the New Age Seduction of Christianity, the infiltration of the Church. Back in England the opportunity to get the answer seemed more remote. But I was reckoning without the Lord. My personal testimony in the year after the visit to America was one of the Lord putting the pieces together. Yet I had to take care I did not become the one deceived. Satan too would be able to weave an interesting pattern if any ground were given to him. Thus I was thrilled when a godly woman made a special point of telephoning me one day. She said the Lord had given her a clear and specific word for me. It was "George and the Dragon." It meant nothing. After a few days there arrived from another source the copy of another article previously referred to. It was called "The Manifest Sons of God". The front cover was dominated by a large and beautiful drawing of George on horseback slaying the dragon. I have referred to the introduction I had to the ministry of Branham; it was quite an extraordinary introduction which I have left for the most part unrecorded. I have already written of what the George-and-the-Dragon essay had to say about this ministry. Now once again I believe God had my attention. The multiple confirmations were anything but contrived by Man. They could not be *natural*. They could not remotely be called coincidence. I believe the Lord used an obedient sister in Christ to show me that it was *not* the "mystery of iniquity" that was at work feeding this material to me.

To this day I fail to see the connection between the Manifest Sons of God and the pictures of George and the Dragon appearing on the cover and in the aritcle itself. Perhaps the penny will drop one day but maybe it has already served its full purpose in my own situation!

Once again a cautionary word is appropriate; the Bible is our guide. It is the clear message of this book that deceptive teachings have come from those who have departed from Scripture. I believe the George-and-the-Dragon episode *was* from God, but whether it was or not, at least we ought not to actively *seek* such leadings apart from His Word. Often coincidences and confirmations may be only what we are looking for subconsciously anyway. As Christians we can be well aware of God's direction in our lives when we *look back* and *review* the path along which He has led us. Except we heed this caution, it can be a short path to believing that the coincidences and experiences of life put us in a special super-spiritual class. All believers are equal before God.

Harnessing the Creator's Power!

The photocopied essay from California bearing the picture of George and the Dragon on its cover introduced me to the second influence (along with Branham's) for the Latter Rain revival at the Sharon Orphanage in Canada starting in 1948. This influence was a powerful book with a powerful title: "Atomic Power with God with Fasting and Prayer" by Franklin Hall. Hall saw the book as one to show the Christian what he called a "sure" method whereby he may "obtain this mighty power" and "be able to move the omnipotent hand of God." The scientists had by 1948 proved the power of the atom with an atom bomb. He had shown his ability, as Hall put it, "to harness the power of the material atom" and now Hall wanted the Christian to use and to "harness the dynamic power of the great Creator of the atom."

Another teaching of Hall's was that the creation was groaning because the sons of God and more of the children of God were not manifesting. He pointed to Romans 8:19:

For the earnest expectation of the creature waiteth for the manifestation of the sons of God.

On Hall's interpretation, the earnest expectation was available now. According to a warning pamphlet issued by the reputed Christian Research Institute (CRI) in America in 1979, all groups that emphasised the doctrine of the manifestation of the sons of God believed that the above scripture referred to an event that takes place in the Church as now established and that the manifested sons of God will still retain the mortal bodies that are familiar to us. Both Franklin Hall, at the outset of the Latter Rain and the revival of Manifest Son's doctrine, and those today who still follow the same path to a misinterpretation of the vital scripture at Romans 8:19, will differ as to details. *When* the event takes place, and what *nature* it will take on, seem, at any rate on the view of CRI in the United States, to be where the differences lie, but these are not usually questions that attract great interest. For many, there is a focus on unity and building the "Kingdom" with little interest in questions of scriptural interpretation. Questions of perfectionism, the perfected Church, and the matter of sin, are ones that follow the misinterpretation of Romans 8:19. The errors pile on top of errors and as the CRI makes clear in its warning paper, the doctrines that have developed from the wrong interpretation have included the merging of Christ's identity with the Church which is pure heresy.

The Manifestation of The Sons of God (Romans 8:19)

Romans 8 presents the whole picture of God's plan for our redemption and verse 19 is our hope and expectation. The earnest expectation of the creation will be answered only by the personal return of Jesus Christ. We shall be delivered from our sinful nature as we put off our mortal bodies and put on our glorified ones which will be like Christ's.

When we become a child of God — when we are saved — we are no longer powerlessly the slaves of sin, but we are still prone to sin. Through the power of the Cross if we *"walk in the Spirit"* we *"shall not fulfil the lust of the flesh"* (Galatians 5:16). We are justified and we are spiritually regenerated when we are saved, and we become a child of God. However there is no basis in Scripture to believe our sin nature will be eradicated before the Lord returns and before being given glorified bodies like His. We look forward to that return and indeed we *do* look forward to the manifestation of the sons of God on that day.

The manifestation of the sons of God we are dealing with

in this chapter is another deception.

Progressive Revelations: Where can they Lead?

One extra-biblical revelation leads to another!

The idea of progressive revelations from God has led some into what is known in America as the Identity message, another deeper realm of revelation where the tribes of Israel have been identified as the Anglo-Saxon races. According to the Christian testimony* of one with first-hand experience in Manifest Sons of God, the essay that was given to me while in America, the groundwork for Manifest Sons introduction into Identity, comprises:

1. Disregard for Israel as the chosen nation of the Jews, emphasising that the Manifest Sons are the true Jews or Spiritual Israel.

2. Belief that Christ didn't have human blood but the blood of God. That's what made Him a Manifest Son of God and when they become Manifest Sons they believe they will also have divine blood.

This would be at the time they rule and judge the world. These ideas usually arise as progressive revelations through those recognised as apostles and prophets.

The British Israelism deception can prove particularly offensive; the tribes of Israel have been identified as the Anglo-Saxon races and this view is sometimes accompanied by violent anti-semitism, the declared need to establish a new world order of theocracy, and the need to cleanse the world of undesirables, most notably Jews. As with most there are depths of the British Israel deception to which some will travel, while others led by the same spirit will not. We wrestle against the rulers of darkness of this world and the same applies to the great men of God past and present.

---

* "An Introduction of the Potential Social Significance of the Manifestation of the Sons of God." (Steve Monterey, USA — 1985)

George Jeffreys

I was saved in an Elim church. George Jeffreys (1889—1962) was the founder of that denomination. He was one of the outstanding revivalists of the age and his great campaigns, particularly in the late twenties and early thirties, packed the largest halls all over Britain winning thousands to Christ and establishing churches throughout the land. Then he came upon the message of British Israelism holding his views on this from about 1920. It is clear from historian Desmond Cartwright's biographical account* that there was no hint of anti-semitism in Jeffreys' reasoning. In those days of the British Empire it was surely easier to believe the lie of a British Israel and George Jeffreys became possessed of a passion to preach it. It diverted his attention not only to the doctrine but to a group of influential and wealthy people from whom support was expected.

I do not know what was the spin-off effect of the error he taught. He left Elim amid controversy but there was none of the spiritual doubt and questioning of his personal healing ministry such as attended William Branham. It is good to give credit where it is due, but more important is the need to hold fast to the truth of the Word of God and receive a warning lesson from Jeffreys' situation. He went off course. The *reasons* can be clear. The *climate* at the hub of a vast British Empire encouraged the error, but the *consequences* a generation later, of a small shift from the truth, can be considerable. This is especially so when endorsed by a man of the stature of George Jeffreys.

God is no respecter of persons. *All* can be vulnerable, and *we* can pray for the Christian leaders who grow up amongst us today. It cannot be too often emphasised in a book such as this one that we wrestle not against flesh and blood but against the wicked powers in the spiritual realm. It is often all too easy to make comparisons in worldly terms. We cannot compare one man's heart to another; we cannot

* "The Great Evangelists — The Remarkable Lives of George and Stephen Jeffreys" by Desmond Cartwright (Marshall, Morgan and Scott — 1986)

compare one man's British Israelism to another. Of course there is a difference between those groups known in America who move in a dangerous kind of Nazi-type anti-semitic direction, and the sort of British Israelism that many such as George Jeffreys profess. In essence British Israelism, whose ideas are promoted today by Herbert W. Armstrong's Worldwide Church of God and "Plain Truth" magazine, holds to the unscriptural idea that Britain and the United States constitute the ten lost tribes of Israel. Many do sincerely believe that, and there is a powerful spirit at work. Satan hates the Jews. He hates God's chosen people. Anti-semitism works in many ways. At its most ugly we need to remember the Nazi holocaust. For my own part, as an unsaved businessman I avoided Israel and submitted to the Israeli boycott and Arab regulations about dealings with Israel in order to protect the valuable oil-related commerce. At another level British Israelism, blind to the identity of the Jew, is anti-semitic too.

George Jeffreys was *not* anti-semitic, but in the supernatural realm, Satan most certainly *is*. Satan works on a broad front with long-term plans. Henry Ford was no preacher but across the Atlantic Satan had a plan for him too. " 'The International Jew' was written by the famous motor car pioneer, Henry Ford, and published in 1920. This gave credibility to The Protocols and because of the Ford name they made a big impact."* The Protocols of the Learned Elders of Zion *were* anti-semitic. Ford had half a million copies printed, and even after he had changed his mind about them and realised his mistake, the powerful idea well promoted in the spiritual realm had taken hold. Hitler picked it up and printed vast numbers of additional copies. It is a message of this book that Satan's intentions for our Christian leaders are far more subtle. I believe the anti-semitic spirit is a powerful one. Jeffreys' *motives,* genuine though they probably were, are irrelevant here. The issue is "truth" and "error". If men allow themselves to reach

* "Understanding the New Age" where further detail can be found.

the heights of one like Jeffreys, what they surely daren't do is to relax for one moment their grip on sound and well-recognised biblical doctrine. The Bible says: *"My people are destroyed for lack of knowledge"* (Hosea 4:6). Jeffreys relaxed that grip. Many leaders today, far removed from Scripture, seem set on refusing to learn a lesson, whether from Scripture or from the sad example of a man like George Jeffreys.

George Jeffreys is but a single example taken from among the Christian leaders of the past. Indeed *all* Christians are examples in the sense that we need *always* to be searching the Bible and measuring up our lives against it.

All enemies have to be put under the feet of the Manifest Sons *before* Christ can return to receive the glorious kingdom *they* have established. That is the message! We do well to remember that Satan blinds slowly; the deeper we will go with him the deeper he will take us for the next step. It is the counterfeit of following Jesus. Some are not yet into the full revelation that Satan would give. Those Manifest Sons who have not yet had contact with Identity would consider not Jews but rather the unbelievers, liberal Christian and politicians, secular humanists, etc as the enemies of God. Renegades at some stage have to be excluded.

Anti-Semitism

In her well-researched book "A Planned Deception — The Staging of a New Age 'Messiah' " Constance Cumbey writes from an American perspective of the way in which the New Age Movement is gaining a *political* momentum with the evident resurgence of a hate campaign against the Jews. She points to the more simple-minded hate groups that have been encouraged by the intellectual occultists. In turn it is propaganda they have fomented that has helped to spur on the Identity movement featuring the various conspiracy theories advanced by the Nazis, themselves established after the New Age pattern examined in "Understanding the New Age — Preparations for Antichrist's One-World Govern-

196

ment.'' In my own reading and research for that book I was for a time not discerning the anti-semitic spirit at work. However through the grace of God I recognised this dangerous thread in the teaching of some who were fighting occultism or who in other ways had valid and sincere Christian ministries.

A document known as ''The Protocols of the Learned Elders of Zion'' was a forgery to bring a deceptive Jewish connection to the conspiracy to rule the world. Powerful occult forces brought this document into focus, long after the forgery was published in Russia at the beginning of this century, and it was instrumental in fomenting the Nazi Holocaust of the Second World War. As Mrs Cumbey points out, what many proponents of the Protocols, many of them Christians, fail to grasp is that the document is a major tool that can be used to bring about the occult domination of society today just as it has been in the past. I do not believe we should ignore The Protocols. Rather we should recognise that they contain within them a plan that goes back to Madame Blavatsky of the anti-semitic Theosophical Society, and most probably beyond that to the foundation of the Order of the Illuminati in 1776. What the Protocols are *not* is a Jewish conspiracy.

The infiltration is subtle. Anglo-Israelism and the teaching that the-Jews-are-not-Israel seem to be powerful tools of the New Age infiltration of the Church, steps along the road to other deceptions. Just how far various victims of deception have travelled we do not know, but this up-to-date testimony of one with first hand experience in the United States tells us:

''Since the Latter Rain Movement and the Manifest Sons of God doctrines are still considered controversial to many Pentecostals and Charismatics, their teachings, and their implications are generally kept underground until one is considered sufficiently spiritual to accept them. This is done through much use of intricate typology, allegory, and symbolic meaning by which many of the deeper truths are implied rather than clearly stated, leaving one to receive the revelation by putting the pieces together oneself. The result

197

is that of a truly esoteric mindset, laden with spiritual secrets and hidden meanings. The analogy of the Outer Court, the Inner Court and the Holy of Holies of the Temple is often given in explanation for these progressively deeper realms of truth. Networking also functions as a means by which the deeper teachings filter down from Manifest Sons to potential Pentecostal and Charismatic converts while maintaining a low profile."* By this means many become involved without realising it.

Getting the Manifest Sons Message over to Charismatics and Pentecostals

It appears that the Manifest Sons message is presented under different labels and the testimony from the United States (drawn on previously) puts it this way: "Since Manifest Sons of God doctrine is often presented under the names of Sonship, the Kingdom message and the Restoration message, it is not always recognised for what it is."* One source provides foundational introduction into Manifest Sons doctrine. Another appears to be central in introducing Manifest Sons' concepts in ways more readily acceptable to Pentecostals and Charismatics, and a white-washed version of Manifest Sons of God doctrine can be seen in the Kingdom message and the Restoration movement looked at in the following chapter.

Let us see how far Manifest Sons doctrine, interpreting the resurrection or redemption of the body through Manifest Sons rather than the Rapture, has infiltrated the Church. When is the rapture of the saints in relation to the Tribulation? It is not long ago that the question being asked was "pre-, mid- or post-trib?" Now the issue is becoming "Rapture or not?". The Bible tells us:

> Then we which are alive and remain shall be caught up
> together with them in the clouds, to meet the Lord in the

* Steve Monterey (1985)

air: and so shall we ever be with the Lord.

(1 Thessalonians 4:17)

The message is found in the Word of God. "The Kingdom Message" on the other hand teaches that the Church must take over the world and establish the Kingdom of God on earth. Only then, they say, will Christ return, not to catch us up "to meet the Lord *in the air*", to take His bride to Heaven; He will return *to earth* to reign over the Kingdom we have established for Him. Kingdom preachers deny they are building the Kingdom on earth but isn't that what they really are doing?

One of the best known leaders and writers from the Kingdom/Restoration movement in Britain puts the position perfectly clearly in a book appropriately called "What on Earth is this Kingdom?" "…. There is no divine escape clause for Western Christians in the Bible. It is a grotesque idea which allows the Jews to be massacred, the Soviet Bloc believers to be imprisoned and tortured, while we 'meet him in the sky'! The rapture is a most agreeable doctrine …. but nothing better than wishful thinking, and must be relegated to the area of myth and fantasy."

Whether we believe in the Rapture or not does not affect our salvation. However, we are in the Last Days with the world in the course of being prepared to receive Antichrist. Accordingly the question of the Rapture, and the vital error in Manifest Sons' teaching on this, becomes of great importance. Why? If the real Jesus Christ is going to catch us up and away from this earth and meet His bride *in the air,* then those who expect to meet Christ with their feet planted solidly *on earth* are unfortunately preparing themselves to meet a false "Christ"! Antichrist will not be an obviously evil ogre with horns, but a man of peace, love, brotherhood, who unites the entire world in a seemingly beautiful ecumenism. Those who teach, as do a growing number of Christian leaders, that we must not 'divide' over doctrine but unite at all cost and take over the world and literally establish God's Kingdom here and now, could discover too late that they have been helping to establish Antichrist's Kingdom.''*

Thus we begin to answer the question: what on earth is this Kingdom? It is an important question. We look more closely at the answers in the next two chapters.

First, let us see how one particularly important "Christian" perspective compares with the kingdom Antichrist is building.

The Secret Kingdom

The constant plea of the Kingdom people that I have heard in 1986 is that we are to get involved in the world. This is in one sense quite right. We are to be salt in the world.

However the Bible says that we are ''in'' the world and we are not ''of'' the world. Certainly our lives are *in* the world. We work, whether it is for a corporation or a hospital, whether we drive a bus or work on the land. Our wives go to the supermarkets. Our children go to the schools. Furthermore the Bible doesn't say we shouldn't be involved in the *government* of these organisations. Yet where is all this leading to in the minds of the Kingdom-builders? Shouldn't we view with some caution the themes I heard at the large Christian festivals I have attended and which are reported in this book? "Get on to the Councils! Get on to the School Governors Board! Do this! Do that! Take the world for Jesus!" I realise of course that only God knows the heart and the same *words* and *statements* have different meanings with different people. However in the remainder of this book, it is my aim that ''Kingdom'' *ideas* should become a little clearer.

Few in Britain know the ordained American Southern Baptist TV star referred to previously and who preaches the Gospel of Jesus, Pat Robertson. He preaches other things too. In America almost every Christian knows him personally

* Letter — Dave Hunt (November 1985)

through the medium of television. Pat Robertson's Christian Broadcasting Network (CBN) and his "700 Club" are popular ministries that can hardly be imagined by those outside the U.S. unfamiliar with Christian TV. A survey commissioned by CBN determined that the "700 Club" was the most popular religious programme in the United States. 19.1% of TV households (16.25 million people) watched part of the programme at least once during a four-week test period. The CBN aim is to bring the Gospel of Jesus into the home and I find nothing to bring question to the sincerity of this intent. Yet they seek also to bring in Christ's reign on earth.

As reported in "New Wine" magazine in February 1986, Christians across America have "begun to realise the necessity" of getting involved in public affairs. According to Pat Robertson, in 1985, the evangelical movement was becoming one of the most powerful forces in American politics. He thinks there are maybe twenty million evangelicals in the Republican Party alone out of a fifty million evangelical population. As referred to in chapter seven, Robertson believes he has heard from God that CBN is to film the Lord's return to earth! The political preparations for this return are evidently in process too. The focus on the need for Jesus and the Kingdom in human hearts and on the return of Jesus IN THE AIR is being increasingly blurred. As Constance Cumbey reasons* (and I present my own reasons throughout this book), this unscriptural earthbound goal is one that could cause much confusion in the body of Christ. New Age forces will be joined up with kingdom-building forces, with Antichrist forces, and from Robertson's own writing we can get a view of the utopia that is expected.

When I was in the United States, I was able to watch Christian TV and buy a copy of "The Secret Kingdom" by Pat Robertson. The cover described it as a national best-seller and, excepting the author's portrait, it contained no sugges-

---

* "A Planned Deception — The Staging of a New Age 'Messiah' "

tion that it was a Christian book. That matters little, but it
alerted me to "eight laws" of the "Secret Kingdom" that
are at work behind all genuine happiness, achievement and
fulfilment. These eight laws are to unlock the door to
unbounded success in business and family life.

I found that the first law was the "Law of Reciprocity".
Robertson identifies seven areas, namely, war, trade,
injustice, crime, pollution, productivity and government, and
he outlines a world view of utopia where men everywhere
would operate on the principle of giving what they expect
to receive. The threat of invasion would be gone and wars
would end. Trade would occur where it was needed without
any "runaway greed". Extremes of wealth and poverty
would be evened out through human generosity and kind-
ness. Prisons would be obsolete. There would be no more
pollution and no more shoddy workmanship. In government,
as men treat each other as God intended, rigid regulation
would be unnecessary and bureaucracy would disappear.

That is a scenario that is quite clear in the minds eye of
New Age people. That is a scenario from one who has the
potential to be — if he is not already — the man we may
call the world's most influential Christian. Pat Robertson is
a serious contender for the presidency of the United States.

All the New Age groups, Greenpeace, CND, and a whole
range of them identified in my book "Understanding the New
Age — Preparations for Antichrist's One-World Government", would identify with Robertson's "Secret Kingdom"
manifesto, his seven areas and his aim for them. As the New
Age of computers, the cashless society and Satan's one-world
government conspiracy described in my earlier book run their
course, isn't it clear that the Church is being infiltrated? Isn't
it clear that many will be wooed from there into the apostasy
of which the Bible speaks to join the New age bride the
Antichrist is preparing?

Some will say: "But how could Pat Robertson's utopia
possibly be achieved?" "How can you take it so seriously?" The answer is that we do so because the scenario
presented by Robertson is little different from what the

Bible describes. It is the scenario of the end-time with a setting of the stage for Antichrist who will come in the flesh. Before considering Robertson's position against the scenario for Antichrist the Bible presents, let us see where the root of the delusion began.

Where then did Pat Robertson first start to go wrong? The answer is usually to be found when we ask the question "what think ye of Jesus?" What view is taken of the word of God? In his TV programme on 1st June 1978 Pat Robertson made the following statement:.

"Anything coming through Man is contaminated to some extent. Therefore, since the Bible came through Man, there must be some errors in it. So we must never equate the Bible with the perfect Jesus."*

We *can* believe the Word of God. Jesus was that Word made flesh.

The Choice: Antichrist's Kingdom or the Lord's?

Firstly let us consider Pat Robertson's solution; *secondly* we shall see what the Bible says.

Having dealt with the relief which the Law of Reciprocity would bring to the major problems of the world, Pat Robertson in the next section of "The Secret Kingdom" turns to one problem he believes would have to be overcome. "Renegades Excluded" is the heading; renegades have to be exluded. He tells us:

"As the renegade gives (living outside law and decency) so will he receive from the entire society in force. He will be ostracised .... For domestic tranquility, there must be a police force and a system of justice capable of bringing sure and swift punishment upon those who rebel against society."**

* as quoted in "Occult ABC" by Kurt Koch (Literature Mission Aglasterhausen Inc. — Germany, 1978)
** "The Secret Kingdom" by Pat Robertson (Bantam Books Inc. New York — 1982) Used by Permission. Thomas Nelson Publishers.

It has already been noted there will be no need of prisons.

Let us now see what the Bible says. We read in Revelation 13 of the Antichrist come in the flesh which the whole world will follow (verse 3). Men will worship the Antichrist (verse 4) and he will bring a time of peace, *".... when they shall say, Peace and safety; then sudden destruction cometh upon them ....*(1 Thessalonians 5:3)

Then we read in Revelation 13:7 that Antichrist will be given power to make war upon the saints (verse 7). He will be given power to "overcome" us (verse7), yet it is all in God's plan ordained from the beginning, and in Revelation 13:15—18 we read:

"And he had power to give life unto the image of the beast, that the image of the beast should both speak, and cause that as many as would not worship the image of the beast should be killed.

And he causeth all, both small and great, rich and poor, free and bond, to receive a mark in their right hand, or in their foreheads:

And that no man might buy or sell, save he that had the mark, or the name of the beast, or the number of his name.

Here is wisdom. Let him that hath understanding count the number of the beast: for it is the number of a man; and his number is Six hundred threescore and six."

As Christians we have to choose. Is it to be the laws of the secret kingdom, or do we choose the Word of God? Are we with the New Age bride or are we the Lord's? Are we building the Kingdom right here on earth or are we looking forward to being caught up with the dead in Christ in the clouds to meet the Lord in the air (1 Thessalonians 4:17) and to receiving our glorified bodies (Romans 8:23)? Will we stand with the Lord, be counted by the world as a renegade and persecuted for Christ's sake, or will we enjoy the peace and utopia of the New Age?

We have a choice; God has given us sovereignty over our free-will and we always have that choice.

More books on
The New Age Movement

"Understanding The New Age - World Government and World Religion"
by Roy Livesey (New Wine Press - 1989) 224 pages **£3.50**
- a **Different** book on "that antichrist", Rome and the Jesuits
- a **Different** look at the Bankers, Credit and the "Love of Money"
- a **Different** perspective on Conspiracy. Wasn't History planned?

"Understanding Alternative Medicine - Holistic Health in the New Age"
by Roy Livesey (New Wine Press - 1988) 224 pages **£2.95**
- a Christian Perspective on New Age Health Care
- an exposé of the occult in Alternative Medicine
- encouraging Discernment amongst Christians

"More Understanding The New Age — Discerning Antichrist And The Occult Revival"
by Roy Livesey (New Wine Press - 1990) 160 pages **£2.95**
- identifying ways individuals are deceived in the New Age
- the move towards a One-world faith
- a Call for Christians to use more Discernment

"The Prince and The Paranormal - The Psychic bloodline of the Royal Family"
by John Dale (1987) 256 pages £3.50
- following the "search" of Prince Charles in the New Age
- a Review of long Royal involvement in the Paranormal
- evidences the need to Pray for our Rulers

"New Age to New Birth - A personal testimony of two Kingdoms"
by Roy and Rae Livesey (New Wine Press - 1986) 190 pages £2.50
- experiences in the New Age and the Occult
- unravelling Satan's Deceptions as a Christian
- cautionary addendum (1989): measuring Experiences and Testimony against the Word of God.

Roy and Rae Livesey also publish **New Age Bulletin**

Personal Orders for the above books, and details of **New Age Bulletin** will be supplied to those who write to Roy and Rae Livesey at Bury House, Clows Top, Kidderminster, Worcs. DY14 9HX. England.

Scripture Index

Subject Index